Fellowship Matters

Andrew Perry

*and they shall spring up as among the grass,
as willows by the water course*

This book is dedicated to

Eileen

Published by:

WILLOW PUBLICATIONS
13 St. Georges terrace
East Boldon
Tyne and Wear
NE36 0LU. U.K.
andrewneileen@yahoo.co.uk

© 2007 Third Edition, Andrew Perry

First Edition 1985,
Second Edition 1996
Third Edition 2007

ISBN 0 9526192 3 7

Other Publications by WILLOW include:

HEAD-COVERINGS AND CREATION
BEFORE HE WAS BORN
DEMONS, MAGIC AND MEDICINE
BEGINNINGS AND ENDINGS

Books available from www.lulu.com\andrewneileen

Table of Contents

PREFACE

PREFACE TO THE SECOND EDITION

CHAPTER ONE   10
Christian Separation from the World

CHAPTER TWO   15
The Basis of Christian Fellowship

CHAPTER THREE   48
The Ecumenical Challenge

CHAPTER FOUR   67
Ecclesial Autonomy and Inter-Ecclesial Relationships

CHAPTER FIVE   105
Ecclesial Discipline

CHAPTER SIX   138
House-Fellowships

APPENDIX A   163
Repentance, Forbearance and Marriage Problems

PREFACE TO THE THIRD EDITION

The changes made for the third edition are a few minor ones relating to errors of grammar and spelling, one or two expansions, and in the layout of the book. I have also removed the index.

PREFACE TO THE SECOND EDITION

When I first released 'Fellowship Matters' as a ring bound volume, it 'fell dead-born from the photo-copier' (Hume). I wrote the study in order to find out for myself what the Scriptures taught about the subject of fellowship, as I was concerned about the divisions that existed between the various fellowships of Christadelphians, and I wanted to determine if these were soundly based.

The original document attempted to reconcile differences of opinion. I took it as a measure of its success the fact that brethren in different fellowships read the book and didn't demur from its contents. This indicated to me that part of the problem with division lies in entrenched ways of looking at things, and if you break out of these ways, you can make progress towards a more united position on the subject of fellowship across the fellowships. However, it is difficult, if not impossible, to overcome inertia and complacency.

This second edition is a complete re-write of the first edition, with a Scripture index added. Much of the new material was released as a series of five 'home-produced' booklets, and which are now out of print. I have added new material on our separation from the world, and the ecumenical challenge to *the truth*, material that first appeared in *The Testimony* magazine.

My aim in the re-write has been to be more *readable and conversational* in the style, with the hope that my points will be made all the clearer. (The first edition was somewhat verbose and long-winded). Those who have the first edition should detect the difference. This edition can be taken as a running commentary on what I was saying in the first edition.

The book begins in **Chapter One** with a brief statement of the principle of separation from the world, a principle based on the fact of our *birth* to another country. From this basis we explore the basis of Christian fellowship in **Chapter Two**. We conclude that the Gospel is the basis of our association. Having identified this basis, our next question naturally concerns other churches. Should we regard ourselves as part of wider Christendom and have fellowship with orthodox churches? This is the *ecumenical* question we address in **Chapter Three**. Our position is that we cannot share fellowship with churches that do not associate on the basis of the same Gospel, baptise into the saving name of Christ, and seek to follow all the commands of Christ.

Having looked outwards, and defined the external boundary of the body of Christ, we turn inwards and consider the relationship of ecclesias in the worldwide body in **Chapter Four**. This is the question of inter-ecclesial unity and ecclesial autonomy. This topic is all about the obligations of the ecclesia to other ecclesias.

Having examined an ecclesia's relationship to the worldwide body, we focus in **Chapter Five** solely on the ecclesia. We detail the practises open to an ecclesia in maintaining the truth. This topic is all about the individual, and the requirements we place on each other in the truth. Finally, we consider the smallest units of ecclesial life - the local house fellowships — in **Chapter Six**.

The structure of the main body of the book is a telescope. We start with the widest perspective — the world — in Chapter One, and then narrow our focus, progressively, until we end up in local houses in Chapter Six. To this structure we have added an appendix: on marriage and divorce, a topic that causes much discussion on fellowship.

Note on versions:

This study is based upon the Authorised Version (KJV) of the Bible. As with all versions, it has good and bad points, but in preparing this book I have been struck time and time again by the way this translation above all others picks up on the nuances, maintains allusions and echoes, and more consistently renders key words with appropriate English equivalents.

The words and constructions of the Authorised Version seem to mirror more closely those of the original languages. This is not only because the linguistic structures of literary language in the England of the seventeenth century were closer to the classical languages. It is also because the philosophy of "word for word" translation underlying the KJV sought to preserve formal equivalence in the translation as much as possible.

All translations are flawed and the KJV is not perfect; it gets the underlying Greek and Hebrew wrong and there are alternatives to consider. I have been mindful of this, and I have used an alternative rendering on some occasions.

Biblical Greek and Biblical Hebrew are dead languages; they cannot change, and to a certain extent this can be said of the language of the King James. The way in which it puts together English words and phrases is foreign to the modern English speaker. The language of the KJV is therefore not only fixed, but it is also separate from the changing forms of contemporary English. So, although we have to make a conscious effort to learn its style, and this is a disadvantage, we gain the advantage of having it insulated from the surrounding forms of English.

Abbreviations

KJV	Authorised Version
O.T.	Old Testament
N.T.	New Testament
LXX	Septuagint
MT	Masoretic Text
GNT	Greek New Testament

CHAPTER ONE

Christian Separation From the World

Introduction
In this chapter[1] we discuss the relationship between the Christian and the world. We approach this by first defining the Biblical basis of the principle of separation to be the concept of **new birth** (Jn 3:5); secondly, we draw out from this basis an additional principle that governs our relationship with the world, namely, that we 'belong' to God. On the basis of these two principles, we conclude that we can have no part in the affairs of the world.

The Principle of Separation
As followers of Christ, our relationship with our fellow man is based upon the principle of separation. This principle can seem a little vague, and difficult to apply. What is separation? Where do we find a description of when or how we ought to be separate from those around us? These are the sorts of question any brother or sister might ask, and they are the first questions of the new Christian life. Our concern in this chapter is to sketch the general principle of separation in respect of the world. In later chapters we focus on the boundaries of fellowship among Christadelphians, and between Christadelphians and the orthodox churches.

The concept of separation has an acceptable and widely accepted meaning that says that a Christian *ought* to separate himself from evil. All kinds of evil present themselves to a modern follower of Christ. The apostle Paul addresses a kind of evil in these words:

---

[1] A longer version of this chapter was a joint piece of work with T. W. M. Evans, and appeared in *For Conscience Sake, The Stand Taken By Christadelphians With Regard To Conscientious Objection To Military Service And Related Matters*, (DCACNS, 1991), and another version appeared in *The Testimony Magazine,* 1990.

> "Wherefore come out from among them, and be ye separate, saith the Lord, and touch not the unclean [thing]; and I will receive you..." 2 Cor 6:17

There are many verses that teach separation from particular things, and this one concerns the worship of idols. However, separation *in general* is based on a different consideration than separation from *particular* evils.

Those who are called by God are his adopted sons and daughters through Christ and they are a separated people. This is shown through the example of Israel, and then explicitly stated by the apostle Peter:

> "For thou didst separate them from among all the people of the earth, [to be] thine inheritance..." 1 Kgs 8:53

> "But ye are a chosen generation, a royal priesthood, an holy nation, a peculiar people; that ye should show forth the praises of him who hath called you out of darkness into his marvellous light." 1 Pet 2:9

As a separated *people* it follows that our citizenship must lie elsewhere other than the area of the world in which we reside. Our *nationhood* is based upon the call of God and our *new birth* in Christ. The logic of this new birth is simple. In the same way that a person is born in a specific country, and he becomes a citizen of that country, so too a Christian's new birth places him in a different nation to the one in which he was born from the womb of his mother (Hebs 11:15-16). With this status, it follows that we are now currently *strangers* and *pilgrims* upon the earth. This was the case with the patriarchs who typify our pilgrimage:

> "By faith Abraham, when he was called to go out into a place which he should after receive for an inheritance, obeyed; and he went out, not knowing whither he went. By faith he sojourned in the land of promise, as [in] a strange country, dwelling in tabernacles with Isaac and Jacob, the heirs with him of the same promise: For he looked for a city which hath

> foundations, whose builder and maker [is] God."
> Hebs 11:8-10

And the apostle Peter, following his statement that Christians are a holy nation, addresses his readers,

> "Dearly beloved, I beseech you as strangers and pilgrims..." 1 Pet 2:11

Like the patriarchs, we are strangers and pilgrims on the earth, and we look for a capital city (of our future country), whose builder and maker is God. Because our citizenship belongs to a future age, and because it has begun now as a result of our new birth, we can have no part in the present order of things, which are to pass away.

In the times of Abraham, a pilgrim or stranger was accorded certain benefits while he stayed within the walls of a city. We ought to have this attitude to the benefits that we enjoy as we live in this world. They are benefits for which we are grateful, but we must not look upon these benefits as 'rights'. As citizens of a heavenly kingdom, we have no rights in the country of our origin or adoption. If we are accorded certain privileges in the mercy of God, then this is something for which we must be profoundly thankful.

> *Acceptance of this Scriptural teaching, that a servant of God is a pilgrim with no permanent dwelling place in the world, should condition our attitude to a whole variety of questions concerning our separation from the world.*

Our separation from those around follows on from our new birth, and so too does the idea of 'belonging' to the God of heaven and earth. If we have been born again through his Word, and if we are his children, then we belong to him *as* children belong to a father. If we have been redeemed by him, then we belong to him *as* a servant to a master. It follows from our 'belonging' to God that we are committed to Him and His commands. This is the presupposition of our lives as Christians. Therefore we must adopt the attitudes that He requires, an attitude He has shown through Christ.

Thus, if God requires us to be separate from the world, then it is a matter for us to find out what this means. So it is that we look to the Bible to find out how, in practise, God has required his servants to conduct themselves among the nations. In carrying out this exercise, we must look at *individuals*, because we are individuals before God. Consequently, we are interested in seeing how God has ordered the lives of His saints of old. But we must also look at Israel, because they were given instructions on how to remain separate from the nations around them. They were just as much a son of God with an obligation to obey God (Hos 11:1).

The essential point is this: separation is woven into the fabric of the lives of all the saints of old, and also God's congregation among the nations, but this separation took different forms. Thus Daniel and Joseph were guided by God to take a position of political office, yet it is also clear how they maintained separation in their lives. Israel, on the other hand, was always counselled to avoid alliances with the surrounding nations. The obvious implication is that God will command His servants and order their lives as He so chooses, for they have chosen to obey only Him.

It is important therefore to distinguish the commands of God. Israel as a nation was commanded to destroy the wicked, but we have been given no such command. *Our* commands come direct from Christ in these matters, and they require us to be as 'harmless as doves' (Matt 10:16) and to not 'resist' evil (Matt 5:39). Christ's commands are the basis of our life of separation from the world.

If we 'belong' to the Father, and if He has given us commands to obey through Christ, then we are responsible to Him for our behaviour. We were created with choice and freewill. This faculty sets us apart from the rest of creation, whose behaviour patterns are determined in advance. We determine our own behaviour. Having been born of God, we should choose to exercise our heart and our senses in His service.

Conclusion
Our separation from society is a large subject, when we consider all the practical details. Our lives intersect with the world in so many ways. After all, Christ requested of his Father that his disciples be 'in'

the world, but not 'of' the world (Jn 17). We have only laid down the first principle of such separation. As Christians, we have been born again of the Word of God (1 Pet 1:23). As newly born individuals, our nationhood is not of this world; it is of another kingdom. A child of God must stick with his Father, his Mother (Gal 4:30), and his family; and keep himself unspotted from this world.

CHAPTER TWO

The Basis of Christian Fellowship

Introduction

We have shown in Chapter One that a Christian is born of the Word and separated from the world. In this chapter we intend to lay bare **the basis of Christian fellowship**. This is a subject that exercises the mind of each generation of believers, and this is no less true today. I offer these thoughts as a basis for answering three questions:

- what is the basis of a Christian church?

- is there a basis for separate fellowships among Christadelphians?

- should Christadelphians be separate from the churches of Christendom?

Each generation of Christadelphians asks: what is the basis of faith? Do we have too much detail? Have we got it right? Are we too strict? Should we tolerate other viewpoints? Should we remain separate from other churches or other Christadelphian fellowships? Many have doubts. A few advocate closer ties with churches. Others are quite firmly in favour of, or firmly against, separation from other Christadelphian fellowships. Considering the basis of fellowship kills our questions with one stone: should we be separate from the churches, and should we be separate from each other in distinct fellowships?

There are many Christadelphian fellowships, mostly small ones, but there is one large central body of Christadelphians, which has been formed over the years by the gradual reunion of once separate fellowships. There are several issues that are usually discussed in and around the subject of the remaining divisions. Briefly, these are:

- the basis of faith
- history of divisions
- ecclesial autonomy
- guilt by association
- inter-ecclesial responsibilities
- block disfellowship
- ecclesial withdrawal
- doctrinal disputes

Here we are looking at the basis of faith (issue one in the list), and the other issues are dealt with in further chapters.[1]

Our view is that separation between Christadelphians and other churches is necessary, while the churches continue to preach fundamental false doctrines, but division between Christadelphian fellowships is a spiritual problem that *urgently* needs to be addressed and resolved. How do we approach this task? It is properly a duty of ecclesial elders in the various groupings, but whoever we are, it is important to hold a correct and balanced doctrine of fellowship, even if this goes against what others say, and to promote this among fellow brethren and sisters.

The Basis of Christian Fellowship

What was the basis of fellowship in the first century? Did the apostles accept just anyone no matter what they believed about Christ? Did they refuse some people on account of what they believed? Did they tolerate moral failures by believers, and still retain them in fellowship? If we can lay down what *they* did in Acts (and the Epistles), we will have a *good* foundation for our fellowship today (Eph 2:20).

---

[1] For example, if someone takes an *ecumenical* line and says there is no reason why Christadelphians can't associate with other 'bible-based' churches, they are not likely to be interested in subjects like guilt by association or block withdrawal, which are subjects that impinge directly on the problem of Christadelphian divisions. We tackle this subject of *ecumenicalism* in Chapter Three.

Why was there a Christian church at all in the first century? There are two points I want to make: the first concerns *beliefs*; the second concerns the *acts* of repentance and baptism.

Specific beliefs were required from people, and only *then* would they have been baptised. If we can find out *what these beliefs were*, we will have an **apostolic** basis of fellowship. The early church came into being because of their distinctive beliefs about Jesus; otherwise, there wouldn't have been a Christian *sect* of Judaism. (Of course the work of Jesus underpins those beliefs). So, if we want to be a church like that of the first century, we too must concentrate on beliefs, and in particular *their beliefs*.[1]

The second point concerns *actions*. When the apostles preached and people were added to the church, certain acts occurred: people expressed repentance; they confessed their belief and were baptised. After this they were regarded as part *of* the church. If we want the same basis of fellowship as the first century, we must believe the things that they believed, we must repent, and we must be baptised. This may appear obvious, but it's meant to be **this** simple. The Gospel is simple, wonderful, and powerful to save a man, *if only* he will listen.

With regard to fellowship and statements of faith, Christadelphians are criticised from two directions:

1. Divisions between Christadelphians occur because of disagreements over procedures, over pastoral matters like marriage and divorce, over points of interpretation in prophecy, and over matters of theology. The dividing fellowships add extra clauses to the previously commonly held Christadelphian statement of faith, and go their separate ways.[2]

---

[1] We **want** (don't we) to be those who follow the apostles' doctrine and *fellowship* (Acts 2:42). The level of knowledge required before baptism, as seen in Christadelphian correspondence courses, reflects the explicit content of apostolic preaching and its implicit assumptions.

[2] By the expression 'common Christadelphian statement of faith' I mean those statements which are consistent with the (B)irmingham (A)mended (S)tatement of (F)aith — *BASF*.

These kinds of division can occur because people lose sight of what the book of Acts is teaching: - belief in the apostles' preaching, repentance and baptism into the saving name of Christ. This will be one of my central arguments in this chapter.

2. But from the outside, Christadelphians are criticised for being too specific and detailed about their statement of faith. In my view the basic statement of faith,[1] which many Christadelphian fellowships share, expresses the things that the N.T. shows as the *content of the apostolic Gospel.* And this will be another key argument in this chapter, aimed at combating the view of ecumenicalism — that Christadelphians should sink their differences and band together with the churches.

Christadelphian fellowships have added supplementary material to the historic statement of faith. They have added doctrines to be rejected and clauses regulating behaviour. For example, clauses have been added stipulating various conditions in cases of divorce and remarriage. This process reflects the apostolic example of combating false doctrine and formulating advice for behavioural problems. But can it go too far? Should such clauses be part of the statement of faith for the whole Christadelphian body, or is there a case for allowing ecclesias to differ on some matters?

It is interesting to read about the history of divisions amongst Christadelphians, and see how the issue that causes a division remains a

---

[1] A recent book, *Studies in the Statement of Faith* (The Christadelphian Office, 1991), discusses each clause of the statement of faith, and is a useful starting point for considering the statement of faith. At least one fellowship, the *Unamended Fellowship* holds to an earlier statement of faith, known as *BUSF*, which has a different formulation to clause 24 of the statement of faith. This clause is about the basis of resurrectional responsibility, but as it stands the *BASF* formulation of clause 24 is formally neutral in its wording vis-à-vis the issues that divide the *Unamended fellowship* from the *Amended (Central) fellowship.* Obviously I can't discuss the details of this disagreement at this point, but clause 24 is about the knowledge that leads to resurrection, and doesn't settle the disagreement, which is about the atonement.

cause of trouble for subsequent generations. Once a division has been set in place, it can be extraordinarily difficult to resolve.

What I have just mentioned above are some practical matters, but there is an important point of doctrine that we should not overlook: *Jesus Christ is the basis of fellowship*. An important passage in this regard, picked upon by the Roman Catholic church, is Matthew 16. In that chapter we read that the church will be *built* by Jesus[1] upon the "rock" of his being the Messiah, the Son of God (Matt 16:16, cf. Jud 6:26). This statement clearly informs us that the basis of Christian fellowship is the truth that Jesus is the Messiah. No other N.T. passage adds to, or subtracts from, this basis (cf. Hebs 6:1, Eph 4). Hence, Paul lays down the foundation of Jesus the Messiah as the only 'foundation' of the church (1 Cor 3:11, cf. Rms 15:20).

It's easy enough to say that *this* truth lies at the root of 'all things', and Jesus did say, 'I am the truth'; but people will say that all Christians believe this, and yet they are divided into hundreds of churches. It is true that one sentence doesn't lay a foundation[2] for men, and so all churches explain what *they* mean by the truth that Jesus is the Messiah, and this is one reason why there are dozens of churches. However, within many churches there are often different groups or fellowships - variations of that church. Among Christadelphians there are different fellowships, yet *they all* substantially agree on the statement of faith that defines the Christadelphian church. So why are *they* divided?

This is the argument I want to develop in this chapter: If we look at what Christadelphians agree upon *generally*, we shall see that it **is** the basis of *apostolic* fellowship (Acts 2:42). With this Biblically authorised basis, why should we *as men* add to the basis, and thereby create subgroups among Christadelphians? Or why should Christadelphians

---

[1] It's easy to forget that *Jesus* builds the church. It's easy to think that *we* build the church, and that Jesus doesn't really have much say in the matter. Unfortunately the ecclesial politics of division can ignore the *fact* that Jesus *has built* a church, since the modern re-discovery of the **mercy and the truth**. It's very easy for men to think that the church is somehow *theirs*, and this can be seen in their writing, for example 'we won't have him at our table' - but it's the table *of the Lord*!

[2] Except for God in Genesis.

give up their statement of faith for wider fellowship with the churches?

The Bible itself contains a lot of detail on what God has required men to believe. You only have to look at the epistles of Paul to see that there is quite a lot of doctrine laid out in ways that are hard to understand. You only have to look at the Gospels and examine the parables of Christ to see their profound simplicity and *yet* also their depth. The prophets and the law also should not be overlooked. The prophets were constantly reasoning with the people about what they should believe, and their language is full of allusions to the earlier Scriptures.

There is therefore much emphasis upon doctrine, fact and detail in the Bible. Hence, we are not being evasive if we say that the Bible itself explains what it means by the truth of Jesus. We might not be evasive, but we might not be helpful. There doesn't appear to be a statement of faith laid out in a series of propositions in the Bible. On the other hand, if you reflect upon the Scriptures, it is possible to set out what *would have been* a first century 'statement of faith'. The early *Apostles Creed*[1] is a later example, and this is similar in its main points to the common Christadelphian statement of faith.

The primary truth that Jesus is the Messiah was the central confession of the disciples; it was the witness of John. But the idea of Messiahship is not just that of kingship and rule, it is also that of suffering and sacrifice. This was Jesus' own thrust in his preaching. He stressed that the Son of Man must suffer and die as a sacrifice for sins. This stress is coupled with his constant preaching about the kingdom of God. Any cursory glance at the gospels will show this to be the case.

> "From that time Jesus began to preach and to say, 'Repent, for the kingdom of heaven is at hand'…"
> Matt 4:17

---

[1] See J. N. D. Kelly, *Early Christian Creeds*, (London: Longman, 1981), 398.

> "Now Jesus went about all Galilee, teaching in their synagogues, preaching the gospel of the kingdom..." Matt 4:23

> "And as you go, preach, saying, 'the kingdom of heaven is at hand'..." Matt 10:7

> "From that time Jesus began to show to his disciples that he must go to Jerusalem, and suffer many things...and be killed, and be raised again on the third day." Matt 16:21

> "To whom also he shewed himself alive ...speaking of the things pertaining to the kingdom of God" Acts 1:3

> "Now I say that Jesus Christ was a minister of the circumcision for the truth of God, to confirm the promises [made] unto the fathers." Rms 15:8[1]

These passages are 'summaries' of Christ's ministry - pointers to the *general nature* of his teaching. If we are going to establish a statement of faith, then it *must* be about the kingdom of God, the promises made unto the fathers, and the death and resurrection of Christ.

In the gospels there are other things that we cannot overlook. There is baptism and repentance - these are *acts* that lie at the heart of the basis of Christian fellowship:

> "Go therefore and make disciples of all nations, baptizing them in the name of the Father and of the Son and of the Holy Spirit, teaching them to observe all things that I have commanded you...." Matt 28:19

This commission of Jesus doesn't mention the Gospel, but it supplies us with a proof text of the crucial role baptism has in the *making* of disciples. It also mentions the importance of observing commands,

---

[1] This preaching evidently concerned *Israel* since this is what the disciples ask of Jesus: 'would he restore the kingdom to Israel?' (Acts 1:6).

for those who are the *newly made* disciples. The commands of Christ then are also part of the basis of fellowship. It seems obvious to say that a Christian follows Christ's commands, but there is a distinction to mark: the commands are *not* the preaching that converts a disciple, rather they show the life to be followed by the *newly made* disciple. Commands define part of the *continuing* basis of fellowship. This is shown in Eden, where God gave Adam a command as a condition of divine fellowship.[12]

The Importance of the Gospel

Christ taught about the kingdom of God and his own suffering. Many of his parables began 'the kingdom of God is like', and his disciples were taught about his suffering. The suffering of Christ is made the centre of the Gospel by the apostles in their epistles and in their recorded preaching in Acts. The issues here concerning fellowship are two:

- Now and again in ecclesial life, the Gospel can get overlooked. Disagreements between brethren often involve details of interpretation[3] and practical matters of how to deal with pastoral

---

[1] This is one reason why christening followed by confirmation doesn't **make** a disciple. If it did, this would be one less obstacle to a wider fellowship. As it is, it has to be wrong to share the body and the blood with those in other churches who are **not** disciples. As ever, apostasy is not blatant but rather a *subtle* counterfeit. An ecumenical approach fails to see this Biblical fact, that false doctrine is a *subtle* variation of truth, for ecumenical Christians admit much *variety* in doctrine. We should *not* allow this - the Bible doesn't make such an allowance.

[2] It follows therefore that a list of commands should be part of the basis of faith, but separated in such a statement from the Gospel. The Gospel makes a disciple and he *enters* the church, while the commands establish his pattern of life and dictate the circumstances under which he might *leave* the church. (I would add also that since the N.T. mentions doctrines to be rejected, there is nothing unbiblical in appending such a list of doctrines in a statement of faith).

[3] It is often said that prophecy doesn't fall within the definition of fundamental doctrine. Since Jesus said that it was not for his disciples to *know* the time of his return, we cannot expect such *prophetic* knowledge to be part of a statement of faith (Acts 1:7).

problems. This has led to block division, but it's important to not overlook the Gospel. If the Gospel is accepted by all parties in a dispute, should they divide on matters outside the truths of the Gospel?

- Between Christadelphians and other churches the disagreement is the Gospel in the first place. So there can be no fellowship with other churches.

If proper **weight** were given to the Gospel in all its doctrinal richness, there would be fewer divisions between Christadelphians.[1] To see this, we have to appreciate the role of the Gospel in *creating* an adopted son of God, and come to see how *such a process* defines the Gospel *as* the basis of fellowship.

What was the Gospel? In Colossians we read that Paul's preaching was about **Christ** (Col 1:27-28). This was his ministry to fully preach the word of God (Col 1:25, A.V. mg.). This ministry concerned the hope of the Gospel, or **the faith** (Col 1:23, cf. v5). The *result* of this preaching was fruit, good works, knowledge of the grace of God (Col 1:6,10), and *participation* in the inheritance of the saints (Col 1:12). Conversion to Christ is therefore bound up with the preaching of the Gospel. The preaching brings forth good works of belief and repentance. We shouldn't therefore *de-value* the Gospel as the basis of what we have in common.[2]

The gospel is what *converts* and *saves*; it is the word of God to create new men and women. In Romans, while talking of his ministry, Paul

---

[1] For example, should divorce be a basis for block division between Christadelphian fellowships, as has been the case? Shouldn't such disagreement be handled within the bonds of the Gospel?
[2] But this happens if Christadelphians separate themselves from one another in large groups, while still believing the same Gospel. For example, disagreement over divorce and re-marriage cases doesn't show that one side has distorted the Gospel. Why then should the parties separate? It's a kind of irony that disagreement about marital separation should lead to separation of fellowship, especially as such fellowship is marital in its typology (See A. Perry, *Head-Coverings and Creation*, (Sunderland: Willow Publications, 1997)

says that the Gospel concerns Jesus Christ, made of the seed of David, according to the flesh (Rms 1:1-4). This Gospel is said to be the *power* of God unto *salvation* to everyone who believes (Rms 1:16-17). In short, the Gospel itself converts people to Christ. Elsewhere Paul declares,

> "...if thou shalt confess with thy mouth the Lord Jesus and shall believe in thine heart that God hath raised him from the dead, thou shalt be saved..." Rms 10:9

This was Paul's calling in the purpose of God toward the Gentiles (Rms 15:16-20, cf. 1 Cor 15:1-2).

Where disunity prevailed, we sometimes read of appeals for unity around this faith in Jesus. Thus Paul beseeches the Corinthians to all speak the same thing, and be perfectly joined together in the same mind (1 Cor 1:10).[1] They were exhorted to be of one mind about the wisdom of God, which he describes as 'the cross of Christ' (1 Cor 1:17), and 'Christ crucified' (1 Cor 1:23, 2:2). Why was this important? It was important because in the preaching of this Gospel there was **real power to save** (1 Cor 1:17, 18, 21, 24). So we read,

- the Gospel is the instrument of birth (1 Cor 4:14-15)

- Christians are born of an incorruptible seed: the word of God, which is preached by the Gospel (1 Pet 1:23, 25)[2]

Moving on from matters of *conversion* to aspects of the day to day, we don't find the Gospel left behind, for Paul worries about the furtherance of Gospel. It was being preached out of contention and out of love. In this situation, Paul exhorts the believers to *stand fast* in one spirit, with one mind, around 'the faith' of this Gospel (Phil 1:27). Elsewhere he teaches that God was *establishing* Christians in the

---

[1] A wider or broader church often allows greater freedom of thought on doctrine, and as a consequence there is less unity of mind. Notice though that Paul sought unity upon the Gospel.

[2] The instrumentality of a word in the new creation is shown in the original creation.

Gospel (Rms 16:25). He stresses the importance of being *grounded* and *settled* in the faith of the Gospel (Col 1:23, 2:7). Accordingly, we read that churches are referred to as *standing* in the faith (Acts 16:5, 1 Cor 15:1).

We haven't yet identified the detailed doctrines of the Gospel, because we must first **lay down the principle that the Gospel is the basis of faith**. It's essential to see that the Gospel is the foundation for fellowship, because it brings a man to new birth in Christ. As we proceed, we will see that the Gospel is not vague and general; the whole of the N.T. belies such a claim. There are quite a lot of doctrines in the Gospel, and these are so intertwined that rejecting one doctrine invariably leads to others being rejected.[1]

So far the Gospel has concerned Christ, rightly so, because he is the second man and the *last* Adam. He is the beginning of the new creation.[2] But we haven't mentioned more than the following propositions:

1. There will be a kingdom of God, which has to do with the promises to the fathers and to Israel.

2. Jesus Christ was crucified as a sacrifice for sins, and raised from the dead.

3. Men and women are saved if they believe in these things and are baptised.

We haven't elaborated upon these propositions, but, if we did, we would see what divides orthodox Christian churches from Christadelphians.

---

[1] In a book like this, I can't discuss the detail of doctrines in any way. There are plenty of Christadelphian books in this area.
[2] This is a crucial point: the first act of God was *creation*; his second act is the *new creation*. The first man of this second creation is Christ, the image of God. Hence he is central to the apostolic preaching. The *woman* of this creation is rightly concerned only with her Lord.

The Preaching of the Gospel
The speeches of Acts are a useful source of the content of the Gospel. In these speeches, O.T. prophecy is tied to recent events, in order to bring people to accept Jesus as the Messiah. With a Jewish audience, the preaching is very Jewish, but this is something that Gentiles need to accept, that ***salvation is of the Jews***. Gentiles need to take on beliefs centred on Israel in order to be saved. One of the problems with the ecumenical orthodox churches is that the Jewish content of the faith is de-valued or altogether obliterated. Here are some of the main points from the early speeches or addresses:

Acts 2:22ff
This speech claims that Jesus was a man[1] approved by God, but delivered up to be crucified. He was raised from the dead, in order to sit on the throne of David. And he is now on the right hand of the Father. It exhorts people to repent and be baptized for the remission of sins, and receive the promise of the Holy Spirit.

It mentions some difficult concepts: predestination, foreknowledge, and miracles. It notes that death could not hold Christ. It mentions the general resurrection and judgement. It mentions the preaching of the Gospel to the Gentiles. It mentions the Holy Spirit.

Acts 3:13ff
This speech mentions the God of Abraham, Isaac and Jacob; that He made a covenant with Abraham, a covenant of the forgiveness of sins; He has raised Jesus from the dead and glorified his son, whom the Jews crucified; it again mentions that this was prophesied by the prophets as part of the process of the forgiveness of sins. The call is made to repent and be converted, in order that sins may be blotted out. It concludes by stating that Jesus will be sent again, when it is time to restore the kingdom to Israel.

It particularly ties the Gospel to the promises made to Abraham, connecting this to the forgiveness of sins. Conviction of sin is a major theme of the apostolic preaching, it was one of the functions of the

---

[1] Dual nature views of Jesus make him both God and man. This is not the testimony of Peter.

Comforter. Hence a doctrine of the devil is integral to the Gospel, as is shown by Jesus' references in his preaching.

Acts 4:8ff
In this short address, Peter preaches that this Jesus of Nazareth, whom the Jews crucified, God has raised from the dead. He is the corner-stone of the temple, and salvation is offered to men only in him.

Acts 5:29ff
This is another short talk. Peter argues that God has raised Jesus from dead, whom the Jews crucified. He has been exalted to be a prince and saviour and give repentance to Israel and forgiveness of sins. And the apostles were witnesses of these facts.

Acts 7
Stephen's defence is an example of the recitation of O.T. history. It's not a form of preaching to the masses, but a defence of the Christian position on the Temple, the Law, and the return of Christ.

Acts 8:30ff
Philip's talk with the Ethiopian eunuch was about Jesus as the fulfilment of Isaiah 53, which means that he must have preached the sacrifice of Christ and the forgiveness of sins. It led the eunuch to confess that Jesus was the Son of God, and be baptized (from Isaiah 53!).

Acts 10:34ff
Peter's speech to Cornelius opens up the Gospel to the Gentiles. He states that Jesus was a man anointed with the Holy Spirit, who performed miracles; he was crucified and raised again by God; he was ordained to be the judge of the quick and the dead; and remission of sins is available through belief in him.[1]

---

[1] That men and women were led to confess that Jesus was the Son of God might strike us as odd. In this day and age, Jesus is **the only realistic candidate** for the title, but in the 1c., it was a real issue as to *who* would be the Son of God.

Acts 13:17ff
Paul's preaching to the Gentiles is similar to that of Peter.[1] At Antioch he preaches O.T. history to the Jewish synagogues, and then connects Jesus to the promises to David. Jesus was the seed that God would raise up in the line of David. This Jesus, he goes on, had been slain by the Jewish leaders in Jerusalem, but God raised him from the dead so that the *sure mercies* of David could be given unto the people, namely the forgiveness of sins. By believing in Jesus they would be justified from all things. This was preaching to a Jewish audience. Paul's preaching to Gentiles started at a different point.

Acts 14:15ff, Acts 17:22ff
At Lystra Paul commenced his apologia with the fact of God and his role as creator of heaven and earth and provider of all good things. On Mars Hill Paul started at the same point. But after setting forth the nature of God, he moves onto the theme of the judgement of the world. This was going to happen because God had raised Jesus from the dead, and he would be the judge.

Acts 24:14ff, 26:2ff
Paul's defences before Agrippa and Felix illustrate important aspects of *his* faith. To Felix he announces that he believed all things written in the law and the prophets, and this he stresses elsewhere on several occasions. (Hence, the spirit of the Law is in the basic Gospel, i.e. the principles of sin, atonement and representation). He declares to him also that his hope was a hope in the resurrection of the dead. To Agrippa he emphasizes the promises to the Fathers, repentance, the forgiveness of sins, and the Messiahship of Jesus as a fulfilment of prophecy.

Acts 28:30-31
Luke summarizes Paul's stay in Rome as taken up with preaching the kingdom of God and the things concerning Jesus Christ.

If we add up the points of these speeches, the content of the Gospel would include: reference to God the Father and Jesus as his Son, the manhood of Jesus and his mortality, the death, sacrifice and

---

[1] Paul's very first preaching was that Jesus was the son of God (Acts 9:20).

resurrection of Jesus, the return of Christ, the promises to Abraham and David, the restoration of the kingdom to Israel, the building of a temple, as well as the general resurrection of the dead and the forgiveness of sins through repentance and baptism.

This is an impressive list of doctrines, and the individual details of the speeches illustrate allusions to many scriptures and make the doctrines more substantial than *my* presentation. Two points can be made:

- the doctrines, as a list, have a **striking resemblance** to the Christadelphian statement of faith

- the preaching of these beliefs preceded baptism and the entry of an individual into the church

Taking the first point, we can contrast these beliefs with many beliefs of the orthodox churches today. The doctrines of the Trinity, heaven-going, the immortality of the soul, the personal supernatural devil etc., are clearly not part of the preaching. Moreover, the *balance of the preaching* is not reflected in many churches. This is because the *Jewish* emphasis upon the promises to the fathers is usually absent in much modern day church preaching. By way of contrast, the common Christadelphian statement of faith is **balanced** in the same way as this apostolic preaching. This common Christadelphian statement of faith contains:

- the foundation is the Bible
- God the Father of Jesus Christ is the one true God
- that man is mortal and sinful and in need of salvation
- Jesus Christ is the fulfilment of the promises to the patriarchs
- Jesus Christ was born of David, a man like his brethren
- that Jesus was a prophet who preached repentance and forgiveness of sins through his sacrifice
- the death and the resurrection of Jesus
- the way of salvation through repentance and baptism
- the kingdom centred upon Israel and Jerusalem

The statement of faith is not just a repetition of the apostolic preaching, because it takes into account the teaching of Paul, but the statement has the same structure as the preaching in Acts.

There is a fundamental connection between fellowship and the Gospel. The apostle John says generally of his preaching: "We proclaim unto you what we have seen and heard, so that you also may have fellowship with us..." (1 Jn 1:3, cf. Is 64:4). The link here is **causal**, i.e. fellowship with John was based on what he saw and heard. He had proclaimed Jesus as the word of life. Christian fellowship is predicated upon the proclamation and acceptance of Jesus. Should we then add to this basis of fellowship with points and details about things not covered by the Gospel?[1]

To summarize our argument, the Gospel is the basis of fellowship for three reasons:

- The Gospel was the content of the apostolic preaching, and therefore the means whereby converts were sought. The Gospel has this structural role in bringing men and women into the church. Hence, it can be claimed to be the basis of fellowship.

- The Gospel (the word) was itself powerful in the conversion process, in the saving of men, and the means whereby men were begotten in Christ. So the Gospel can be said to be the basis of fellowship, because it has an instrumental role in the process of salvation.

---

[1] For example, should we add to the *basis of fellowship* certain clauses about choices in ecclesial discipline. Should we do this if it doesn't feature in the N.T. proclamation of the Gospel? If we do this, what does this say about how we see the Gospel? Do we see the *making* of a disciple as involving the Gospel **and** supplementary views on matters of discipline? Such clauses are often *right* in what they say, but should they be part of a basis of fellowship? The same question can be posed about details of atonement theology and details about prophecy, which are the things of maturity, and very often too difficult for many to understand.

- The Gospel of 'the faith' is independently described in a way that shows it acts as a foundation amongst true Christians. Thus, we have noted that believers are to stand in the Gospel, be grounded and settled in the faith, and that God is establishing Christians in the Gospel.

The basis of fellowship was the Gospel, and we can recover this from *Acts*. Once we know the Gospel, we can recover it from all parts of the Bible, and we needn't start especially with *Acts*. But my argument has stressed *Acts* because I have been concerned with the *fellowship of the apostles* (Acts 2:42).

This conclusion marries well with our interpretation of Matthew 16. Jesus stated that **he** would build the church upon the 'rock', or the truth of Peter's confession, which concerned his Messiahship. We have then two independent lines of evidence for identifying a valid basis of faith and fellowship today, and let us not forget that it is Christ who builds the church even though it may appear to be the work of men.

Repentance and Baptism

As yet, we have made little mention of repentance (Acts 24:25) and baptism, and their relationship to matters of fellowship. We must now redress this omission.

The idea of repentance introduces the moral, the ethical, and the practical into our discussion of fellowship. Repentance is always required from a person before he becomes one with Christ. It is followed by belief and then baptism:

> "Then Peter said unto them, Repent, and be baptized every one of you in the name of Jesus Christ for the remission of sins, and ye shall receive the gift of the Holy Ghost." Acts 2:38, cf. 3:19, 20:21

Why must people repent? Perhaps this is a silly question. But many people visit a church to be christened, to be married, and to be buried. For them, repentance isn't a part of 'being a Christian'. Why isn't this nominal allegiance enough?

The ultimate answer must be found in the account of the Fall. Because man sinned and rebelled against God, He has required men to acknowledge that they are sinners and turn away from sin as a condition of His accepting them. Because God is a righteous God, He cannot allow sin, and so repentance is necessary. Because of this, repentance is a fundamental feature of the purpose of God.

What is repentance? How do we judge genuine repentance? What conditions do we lay down for repentance? Are there only absolute conditions, or is there room for human weakness and individual judgement? Why is baptism necessary?

The command of Christ was to baptize and thereby **make** *disciples. He that believed and was baptized would be saved (Mk 16:16).*

Consequently, we read of several cases where baptism was an integral part of the means whereby converts were inducted into the church: see Acts 2:37,38, 41, 8:4, 5, 12, 36, 38, 9:17-18, *and so on*. The doctrine of baptism is explained by Paul in Romans 6. Here Paul shows that believers avail themselves of Christ's death in baptism, and identify themselves with new life in Christ. As many as are baptized into Christ, these put on Christ in baptism (Gal 3:27). This shows why, for the present time, baptism is essential. It illustrates both the destruction of the old creation, and the emergence of a new creation out of water. In Genesis 1 the pattern was laid down, in the N.T. we see its fulfilment.

Belief, repentance, and baptism were the means through which converts became part of the church.[1] Hence, *all three* elements constitute the basis of Christian fellowship. This implies that Christians would have been united upon these things: belief in Jesus' Messiahship, repentance and baptism into his body.

> *It follows that those who do not practise believer's baptism into Christ, as many orthodox churches do not, cannot be part of the body of Christ. The disciples of Christ cannot look upon these*

---

[1] I am concentrating on just the historical explanation. So it is that I am overlooking the call of God.

> others as *'Christians'*, even though they apparently talk the *'same'* language.

Christadelphian fellowships baptize on the same basis as the original apostles, however, they are divided from each other on various other matters. When an individual moves from one fellowship to another, re-baptism is not required. Each fellowship accepts Christadelphian baptism *per se* as a valid baptism (*a making of a disciple*). The question arises therefore whether the fellowships should be so divided?[1]

In these terms, the various fellowships are divided mainly on how the theology of Paul is to be understood in respect of the atonement, and/or various practical matters of ecclesial and personal behaviour. In addition there exist groupings within fellowships based around some doctrines such as the doctrine of the Holy Spirit.

In thinking about this *Christadelphian situation*, let us consider the preaching of the apostles. This preaching was to bring people to accept Jesus as the Messiah, the Son of God (Acts 2:36, 5:42). Modern day Christadelphian preaching reflects a similar pattern. This latter-day preaching, however, doesn't concentrate on the issues that divide Christadelphians, and this is because Christadelphians substantially agree on a common statement of faith. This shows that, like the apostles, Christadelphians value the Gospel, and recognize that it is a power unto salvation. By concentrating on the Gospel, as the means to bring people into the modern church of Christ, Christadelphians of all fellowships deny, in the very *practise* of preaching, the issues that divide the fellowships. These issues are usually mentioned (if at all) at a very late stage in the making of a disciple, and this shows that they are *irrelevant* to the making of a disciple.

The question should be put as to whether Christadelphians are right to remain separate from each other, when they share a common Gospel, and when they share a common method in the making of a disciple. Should not the differences that exist on practical matters be

---

[1] Christadelphians will rejoice when a person is baptised, regardless of what fellowship administers the baptism. This shows *where their heart is*, even though they are in separate fellowships. We are all a mixture of flesh and spirit.

handled *within* the overall unity of the body of Christ, for example, on a local ecclesial basis? After all, these are matters which only arise for those who are **already** baptised. This is an important point: should Christadelphians be divided on practical matters, especially when they are complicated by many factors.

In the case of some Christadelphian fellowships there is therefore a formal contradiction at the heart of their fellowship. They accept the baptism of other Christadelphian fellowships, for members are not re-baptised when they arrive from another fellowship, but they do not fellowship other fellowships. The point here is: Why not?

A valid baptism into Christ follows belief and repentance. Each modern day ecclesia of whatever fellowship administers this according to the common Christadelphian statement of faith. Some fellowships also impose other beliefs, for example in respect of divorce or the theology of the atonement. But these fellowships accept the baptism of other fellowships. The question arises therefore as to what baptism into Christ *really means*? Is it really *baptism into Christ*? Does it entail that a newly baptised convert is thereby in fellowship with the Father and the Son? If this is true at the point of baptism for all Christadelphian fellowships, and their respective baptisms, why are there fellowships who do not fellowship those who are in fellowship with the Father and the Son in other fellowships on the basis of the apostolic Gospel?

Christadelphian fellowships cannot reply that they do not **know** whether those in another fellowship are in fellowship with the Father and the Son, and therefore must remain apart, for they *already* accept the baptism of the other fellowships as valid. A *valid* baptism must place a person *in Christ* and in fellowship with the Father and the Son in the first instance.[1]

When a judgment is uncomfortable, one course of action is to avoid making the judgment. This can be achieved by saying, 'I do not *know*

---

[1] A fellowship could reply that the baptism was valid, but the person so baptised *might* become out of fellowship with the Father and the Son at the first breaking of bread, because he broke bread with an erring fellowship. This would make the fellowship with the Father and the Son a very brief one indeed!

enough to make the judgement.' Sometimes we may not know enough to make a judgement either way in a certain matter; however, where we have knowledge, we should not duck our responsibilities. We have knowledge of the basis of faith - it is the Gospel - so we cannot put this aside when making judgments about fellowship.

We cannot make a decision to remain separate from a fellowship, when it is grounded in the Gospel. We cannot make such an important and wide ranging decision, when there is a crucial element of doubt, an 'I do not know'. We cannot take a course of action in the absence of any knowledge, there has to be sufficient knowledge to justify the reasonableness of the action.

Where there is apostasy, then *we know* that light has no fellowship with darkness; but notice, this is something *we know*, there is no doubt. Biblical examples of separation all proceed on the basis of knowledge; they don't proceed on the basis of a judgement like: *it might be best to steer clear of those people, even though we don't know whether fellowship with God is affected*. In the Bible, many matters of fellowship were handled within the orbit of the community. These were matters of individual withdrawal, seen both in the Law and the N.T. epistles. They were matters for local ecclesial judgement and discipline.[1]

Actions should be based on **knowledge**. Where we have doubt, we should leave this to the Judgement Seat. In the case of fellowship, it is not that we don't know the basis of fellowship, and therefore the basis of separation. We do: the basis of fellowship is the Gospel. Instead of dividing when we don't know *if* fellowship with God is affected, we should remain united *if* we don't know fellowship with God is affected.

Many (but not all) Christadelphian ecclesias, mainly in the largest body, would fellowship sound brethren and sisters from other fellowships. However, this is generally not the case with the smaller

---

[1] In Deut 17:8, there is a law for hard judgements. How is this applied? If we apply this at the ecclesial level, the case law could vary over time according to the wisdom of the Priests and Levites. What sort of issues might we allow there to be differences of judgement in the application of the law?

fellowships that remain divided from the larger body. What is the more correct practice? Is it to extend fellowship to individual Christadelphians, no matter what fellowship, provided they believe the Gospel? Or is it better to only extend fellowship to those in one's own fellowship? There are many ecclesias in the largest body which follow this exclusive approach, while the smaller fellowships *as a whole* exercise this exclusive approach.

What happens with the exclusive approach is that a member of one fellowship cannot break bread in another fellowship, although he can do all other things: he can run study days, speak at Bible Classes, write for magazines, etc. It could be asked therefore what makes the breaking of bread the touchstone of fellowship. Should an exclusive approach allow members to have *any* fellowship at all outside their own fellowship?

We should identify with the Gospel of Christ; we should proclaim this Gospel and assemble on the basis of the Gospel. We have found it necessary to coin the term 'Christadelphian' to name our assemblies. Since the word means 'brethren in Christ', we are rightly loyal to this identity. But over and above this loyalty, the various small fellowships of Christadelphians are loyal to the reasons that led to their existence. The question is: were these reasons soundly based, or are they an implicit denial of the truth that the Gospel is the basis of fellowship?

The Promises to Abraham
Jesus Christ is the basis of fellowship. But Jesus was a Jew. Why was it necessary for Christians to incorporate themselves as a separate community apart from Judaism? Why did the religion of Christ come about? The answers to these questions are complex, but we can briefly illustrate one line of explanation.

Christianity is a world religion now, albeit largely apostate. Social scientists view Christadelphians as a sect of this world religion. In the eyes of the first century politicians (rulers, administrators, clerks), and also the Jews, Christianity was a sect of another *distinct* world religion -

Judaism. It was the sect that happened to believe that a certain Jew, Jesus of Nazareth, was the Jewish Messiah.[1]

In view of this fact, we can ask quite reasonably, why did the early Christians incorporate themselves into a separate community? The answer lies in considering the doctrine of the unity of Jew and Gentile in Christ. The mystery of God's will was that He would gather together in one all things in Christ (Eph 2:12, 2 Cor 1:21), in order that the Gentiles should be fellow-heirs, and of the same body, and partakers of the same promises with the Jews (Eph 3:6). This was the ministry of the Gospel (Eph 6:19) to the Gentiles.

Why is there such stress on the *unity* of Jew and Gentile in Christ? Why is it an *exclusive* unity? The answer lies in the Abrahamic promises: these are singular in reference - it was to be in **one** seed that all nations of the world would be blessed (Gal 3:24ff). As many as had been baptised into Christ, such had put on Christ, and such had become one with him, and thus heirs to the promises. This is the same as saying that *in Christ* all the promises of God are Yes!, and that it is necessary to be *in him* to partake of them. As Paul elsewhere expresses the point, it is in Christ that all shall be made alive (1 Cor 15:22). Or again, as Peter says, there is no other name under heaven whereby men can be saved (Acts 4:12).

There is then a **principle of association** embodied in the Abrahamic promises, namely, that men and women *are* being associated in Christ in order to partake of the promises. This *principle* impacts upon the question of fellowship and divisions. If Christadelphians are *together* heirs of these promises, **necessarily** in Christ *together*, in order to partake of the promises, can they realistically separate from each other *in blocks*?

---

[1] If we compare Christianity with the first century Jewish sect of the Essenes, we can see that whereas we in the twentieth century take Jesus' Messiahship for granted, this was a substantial and original claim in the first century, which many first century Jews would not have accepted for religious reasons.

If Christadelphians do not associate with one another, doesn't this divide the fellowship of the mystery (Eph 3:9-11), to which fellowship **God** (*no less*) has called us through Christ?

The Body of Christ
The Abrahamic unity in and around Christ is reflected in the teaching about the **body of Christ**. We can see this in the parallelism of ideas between 'in Christ' and 'body of Christ', see Figure 1. A primary aspect of the doctrine of the church as the body of Christ is that the body is *Christ's body*. And as the body is naturally one, and has many members, and all the members of that body, being many, are one body, so also is Christ (1 Cor 12:12). **God** tempers the body together in order that there should be no division in the body, but that the members should care for one another,[1] and share suffering and honour with one another.

Of course, the designs of men can frustrate the work of God, but His intention is that there should be no division (1 Cor 12:24-5). The body has its uncomely parts, but these are necessary, and the body has its feeble parts, but these too are necessary. God puts these parts together in His wisdom, and consequently, the parts are not to say to one another, "I have no need of you" (1 Cor 12:21-23).[2] These exhortations are set in the context of the divisions of the Corinthian church, which was made up of a number of churches scattered around the city, a situation we find repeated today in cities where there are several Christadelphian fellowships.

in Christ	*in one body*
put on Christ in baptism (Gal 3:27)	baptised into the body of Christ (1 Cor 12:13,27)
in Christ, neither Jew nor Gentile (Gal 3:28)	Jews and Gentiles are part of the one body (1 Cor 12:13)

---

[1] The one another virtues of the Christian life stand at the heart of practical fellowship, and it is the practise of *love* which gets hit first when brethren and sisters divide.
[2] Do some divisions reflect the attitude, 'I have no need of you'?

in Christ	*in one body*
Jesus is making out of Jew and Gentile one 'new man' which we 'put on' (Eph 2:15, Col 3:10-11)	
Believers are to walk in Christ, root themselves in Christ, and be built up in him (Col 2:6-7)	Believers are nourished and ministered to in the body, and in the body they are knit together growing with the increase of God (Col 2:19)

It is to a local community in a city that Paul says, "You are the body of Christ", and, "individually members of it" (1 Cor 12:27). However, this refrain can also be found addressed to the Romans, where the body of Christ is thought of in *larger* terms:

> "So we being many, are one body in Christ and every one members of one another" Rms 12:5

The importance of this analogy is wholly *practical*. Fellowship is first and foremost a practical ministry of love, and not a theoretical doctrine. The *local* community should think and act as a body of Christ, while recognizing that they are part of a wider body of Christ.

The body needs to be built up. This is essential for growth. There needs to be unity for this to happen. The members of the body should be joined together serving one another. It is a fundamental error which Paul warns against, when a body does not hold to the *head* from which *all* parts of the body receive their nourishment (Col 2:19). To repeat: there is one head, not several; there is one body knit together, not several; *all* hold to this same head, not just some; and the growth comes from the head ministered through the parts of the body. If the parts break off, the growth is likewise impeded.

In another analogy, Paul states that believers are to be a building fitly framed together growing into a holy temple in which God may dwell (Eph 2:20-22, cf. 1 Cor 3:10). It goes against God's will, when men make the building not fit together. This affects the growth and nourishment of the whole living temple. But this growth and continued *life* is **the purpose of life in Christ**. We grow together, we take nourishment together, we live together.[1]

Those who facilitate growth in the body of Christ include elders, and teachers. These build up the body, in order that it might grow up unto the head who is Christ (Eph 4:1ff, cf. 5:23). But it is just as much the function of the whole body to make increase of the body, to build up the body in love (Eph 4:16), and this growth is from God (Col 2:19).

With such a stress on unity, is there any place for division? The N.T. epistles show many ecclesial difficulties. This is the *normal situation*, against which the faithful must battle. Division is not the first response to error and waywardness. For example, the churches in Asia Minor at the time of the seven letters showed considerable ecclesial problems. Christ addressed the churches, and still regarded them as in his hand, but the warning implicit in these letters is plain: if repentance was not forthcoming, some individual ecclesias would be removed from their position. There is therefore a place for separation, and this should take place against ecclesias which forsake the practise of the faith and refuse correction by local sound ecclesias. Such an eventuality is serious, and not to be undertaken in a pre-emptive manner. While we need to take on board the long-suffering of Christ in his own approach to the Revelation ecclesias, we need to recognise that for comparably serious situations ecclesias may need to be placed outside the body.

The Commands of Christ and Repentance

Christ said, 'Ye are my friends if ye do whatsoever I command you' (Jn 15:14), and those who seek to be his friends strive to obey his commands, whether these were delivered by their Lord, or by his apostles.

Some of the commands are black and white, but those who have been baptised into the one faith have disagreed amongst themselves on some of the commands. The major area of dispute has been in respect

---

[1] It is interesting to observe that across all Christadelphian fellowships there is much sharing of *written material* regardless of the fellowship of origin. This is one way in which the body of Christ as a whole is being ministered and knit together despite the continuing divisions.

of marriage and divorce, and in the conditions of repentance to be applied in the case of marital failures. Other topics of disagreement have concerned such things as breaking of bread arrangements, the use of the divine name, the use of Bible versions, and so on.[1]

In respect of divorce and re-marriage, the commands under dispute have not been whether it is wrong to get a divorce or to re-marry. All Christadelphian fellowships accept that the ideal is one man and one woman for life. The issue has been *what to do* with regard to those who fall short of this ideal and seek a divorce, and thereby put asunder the marital partner, and then possibly re-marry; or *what to do* with those who seek more than one marital partner, say in an African country. What should be done where there is 'repentance' of the actions taken?[2]

Repentance is important to fellowship matters because, as we have seen, repentance was one of the three parts to the first century basis of fellowship: repentance, belief and baptism. There will always be disagreement on this question of repentance. It is not the purpose of this chapter to examine the issues and propose some general doctrine of repentance and marital failure.[3] Brethren will adopt one of two approaches to repentance: they will either insist on complete forsaking of the state of divorce or re-marriage, or they will *suffer* some degree of incompleteness in the repentance. What should brethren of Christ do when they disagree over the conditions of repentance (or a command)?

Two main courses of action have been followed when brethren of Christ have disagreed over the *application* of a command (e.g. the

---

[1] Other commands which might be cause for disagreement might be those to do with military service. Should a brother take part in combat? Other commands might be to do with police service, and the use of force. I say these might be a cause for disagreement, but it's not clear whether they are presently issues of concern. Military service and police service are excluded in an appendix to *BASF*.
[2] In our dealings with each other we should reflect the *longsuffering* that God has shown towards his children, or the *longsuffering* Paul showed towards his children, or the *longsuffering* we show towards our children.
[3] See Appendix A.

command to repent) of Christ. One course has been to split the body of Christ globally and put into place new structures mirroring the old structures. This has been known as *block division*. It essentially sets up a **new church**. The essential characteristic of this process is *autonomy*. The new fellowship becomes an autonomous unit in respect to the old fellowship. Both fellowships co-exist across the globe (theoretically), but each is autonomous in respect to the other, i.e. there is ecclesial autonomy. (Remember Israel were only *one* ecclesia in the wilderness).

Another course of action that has been followed has been to restrict the autonomy to *local* ecclesias. With this course of action, ecclesias are left free to determine *autonomously* the application of the disputed command of Christ - to forbear, or to insist on complete obedience on a matter. It's not that a command is rejected by some and accepted by others, but rather the problem almost always concerns how to deal with a failing person.

In both *fellowship autonomy* and *ecclesial autonomy* a measure of autonomy based around *an* **ecclesial unit** is introduced in order to allow the disagreement to be handled. In the one case the ecclesial unit is a *new global fellowship*, in the latter case it is an *existing local fellowship* (ecclesia). Both processes share the same strategic logic. Unfortunately, the phrase 'ecclesial autonomy' has been introduced to refer to only *local ecclesial autonomy*, but the situation really requires recognition that *autonomy* is operated at both levels. For example, currently there are several distinct *global fellowships* separated on matters of divorce and re-marriage, and associated views on the conditions of repentance; but there are also fellowships that argue that this has drawbacks and operate *local autonomy* in respect of divorce and re-marriage, judging problem cases on their merits and de-merits.

Christadelphians, no matter what fellowship, are separated from other churches, and this is a *global* separation. The bases of this separation are the fundamental differences that exist on the nature of God and His Son, and about the Gospel. Where there are fundamental doctrinal differences, there must be separation of the community of Christ. We have seen this in connection with the first century, where the early Christian ecclesias were separated from the system and doctrines of the Jews. Those who worship God must worship Him in spirit and in truth.

> *Should this global separation, which we can see at a level between Christadelphians and other churches, be duplicated where there is disagreement between Christadelphians over the application of the commands of Christ, such as those about divorce and re-marriage or the doctrine of resurrectional responsibility?*

What does *global separation* mean? In the case of the orthodox churches, it means there is no satisfactory basis of common worship and service of God and Christ. Orthodox churches worship a Trinitarian God; in many cases they do not practise baptism into Christ; the Abrahamic Gospel is not preached in other cases, *and so on.*

When Christadelphian ecclesias separate on a *global basis*, what does this mean? How does this work out? It means that a common recognition of the unity of God, of the doctrine of God-manifestation, of the nature of Christ, of his sharing our nature, of our mortality and sin-proneness - that this is not enough for common fellowship; it means a common understanding of the promises to Abraham, Isaac and Jacob, and to David, these are not enough for fellowship; it means that a common understanding of such things as the devil, the resurrection and judgement, the future place of Israel in the purpose of God, and the millennium, these things are *not enough* for fellowship.

When there is **all this** (and more) in common, what does a process of *global dis-fellowship* mean, over say the conditions of repentance for divorce and re-marriage? It means that those things that constitute the Gospel and the power of God to save are not actually *enough* for fellowship! It means, for example, that *complete agreement* over divorce and re-marriage is *essential* to fellowship. The very process seems to de-value the Gospel, and elevate the ideal of *complete agreement* on all practical matters of spiritual wisdom. In fact, it seems a **massive** *de-valuation of the Gospel*, as **the** basis of *conversion*.

On the other hand if Christadelphian ecclesias disagree over the application of a command of Christ, and separate *locally*, on an *ad hoc* basis, what does this mean? It means there is a lack of unity on the matter concerned, but this has not extended to the Gospel. Such local dis-unity produces a messier state of affairs, but this is to be expected. What contacts continue to exist between the ecclesias will vary, depending on the strength of feeling. There may be inter-ecclesial fellowship in respect of preaching and fraternals, or a sharing of common visiting speakers, and so on. On the other hand there may be no contact at all between the ecclesias. Nevertheless, both ecclesias will be formally in the same fellowship, and duty bound to address the problems in their dealings with one another, whereas formal global divisions allow men to ***forget*** those from whom they are divided.

It is important to reflect the Bible in our actions. We have to recognise the importance of the Gospel, but disagreements tend to overshadow this shared basis of faith. We can't avoid disagreements; neither can we avoid local ecclesial troubles. All we can do is work *through* the tribulation that they involve, while holding to the Gospel.

How has God dealt with apostasy? In the case of Solomon's apostasy, the kingdom was divided administratively, but this division did not extend to a division of the community with regard to the religious fellowship of the community at Jerusalem. It was Jeroboam who fractured the religious worship at Jerusalem with the introduction of the golden calves. Is there anything to learn in this angelic example?

What does the N.T. indicate? Are there *block disfellowships* in the N.T.? There appear to be one or two. Paul separated the disciples from the Jews in Ephesus, when the Jews did not believe and spoke evil of the Way (Acts 19:9). This was a *local* case of *en bloc* separation. In Antioch Paul withstood Peter for separating himself from the Gentiles on account of the 'circumcision fellowship', for he was to be blamed (Gal 2:11-12). (The problems with the circumcision fellowship were eventually addressed by the *re-union council* of Acts 15.) There were divisions at Corinth, which Paul condemned (1 Cor 1:10).

Apart from these cases, the overwhelming evidence of the N.T. is that the ecclesias were in various states of spiritual health.[1] There is no

---

[1] If we take a time-slice of the first century fellowship of the apostles, and we imagine them as a Christadelphian fellowship, how would they

evidence of the practise of *block withdrawal* or the setting up of separate fellowships. The practise of withdrawal and ecclesial discipline was administered at the *local* level.

The commands of Christ are part of the basis of fellowship, because they are part of the *entry* requirement into the body of Christ that a person repent. However, the commands of Christ require continual practise, and failure is inevitable. The issue becomes to what extent we tolerate *failure*, and to what extent we apply ecclesial discipline. This is an issue which concerns the possible *exit* of a person from the daily life of the ecclesia. God sets a high standard, and we all fail to reach this standard: "Be ye therefore perfect, even as your Father which is in heaven is perfect" (Matt 5:48). Unless God will tolerate our achievement of a lower standard, none will be saved. The principle[1] of remitting sins today (John 20:23) has an *analogy* in our administration of *forbearance* towards each other by helping each other in our failures. If we do this, we will be seeking to imitate the example of God in Heaven, who was abundant in long-suffering to the fathers as well as the children when they failed. However, if we do not also exercise discipline and mark out the boundaries of acceptable behaviour, we will also fail in our duty to reflect God. It is a matter for local judgement.

Conclusion

I hope this chapter presents a balanced case. There are many other things that can be said in a fuller treatment of these things. I have

---

be viewed as a whole? Christadelphian fellowships have been known to divide and remain separate from each other in *far less* circumstances than those of which we read in the N.T. letters. I can imagine Twenty First Century Christadelphian fellowships saying to the First Century fellowship: 'We'll have nothing to do with you until you sort yourselves out'.

[1] This principle is based on analogy with Exodus 23 and the activity of the Angel of the Presence; it places the disciples into an analogous role of leading the church through the wilderness. If this principle has an application today, it is in the area of ecclesial discipline; I am not presenting the view that the Holy Spirit is possessed by believers today, neither do I think that we 'forgive' the sins of others, except personal offences against ourselves.

endeavoured to show that the Lord Jesus Christ is the basis of fellowship, for Christians are essentially baptised *into* Christ. This is the doctrine of Abrahamic unity in Christ, and it implies that Christians are to associate with one another. This is developed in the pastoral analogy of the *one* body of Christ in which Christians show their day to day love for one another.

Division amongst Christadelphians is contrary to this principle of association around Christ, and contrary to the principle of togetherness in the body of Christ. The basis of this unity is the Gospel, because this is the power of God unto salvation; hence, it was the basis of apostolic preaching. Insofar as Christadelphian ecclesias hold the Gospel, they should associate with one another.

The extent to which Christadelphians tolerate failure in their brethren and sisters, the extent to which they accept that a person has repented and is genuinely seeking to return to the Lord Jesus Christ, these have been matters for disagreement amongst brethren. This has been so because they are the judgements of practical wisdom 'in the gate'. There will be differences in these things, but these differences should be handled *within* the community, because they are not differences that amount to apostasy.

Is uncertainty at the root of our fellowship with each other? Are there no criteria or fruits by which we can determine the disciples of Christ? Did Christ say that it was by fruits that a tree was known? Did Christ not say that his disciples *would be known* if they obeyed his commands? Are there not an abundance of passages designed to give us confidence that we both know the truth, and know that we are of the truth, and know also that we fellowship those who know the truth (e.g. 1 John *passim*). If we *can* know the disciples of Christ, then are the fruits of a disciple, are the commands upheld by a disciple, not in evidence amongst all Christadelphian fraternities? If this is the case, and if God is calling men and women through all fraternities, is the present divided state of the brotherhood something to be undone before the return of Christ?

A balanced doctrine of fellowship will embrace the whole of the Scriptures. We all fail to understand, but we must fight this; we must fight the complacency. We must continually grasp the Gospel, rejoice in its power and no matter what our internal troubles are, we must never let the preaching of this Gospel to others outside be diminished. It is the power of God to those who desperately need salvation.

CHAPTER THREE
The Ecumenical Challenge

Introduction
The title of this chapter is provoking. Orthodox Christians in many churches have argued for ecumenical fellowship amongst their denominations. The challenge to Christadelphians is that they should lower the barriers of fellowship, and seek to share worship with other churches. Our purpose is to examine the nuts and bolts of the reasoning that leads to this sort of proposal. Our focus is not some individual or group within the community, such identify themselves, but rather our aim is to examine the kinds of argument that lead individuals to entertain wider fellowship. What then is the challenge?

Aspects of the Challenge
The problem is one of **similarities and differences**. Those who favour an ecumenical approach, point to similarities between Christadelphians and orthodox churches.[1] The following points are examples of propositions used to support ecumenicalism:

- The language of Christian worship is much the same between the churches of Christendom and Christadelphians. Many hymns are the same, and the forms of address in prayer are similar. *It's the same God, so why can't Christadelphians go to other churches for worship?*

- The Bible is understood to be the inspired word of God in many churches, and it is the general basis of church life. *So why can't Christadelphians participate in other churches' bible-based activities?*

---

[1] My knowledge of the orthodox churches is both by experience, attending ministerial training courses, talking with others, and by reading, and it is limited to such U.K. churches as the low church of England, the Baptist church, Pentecostals, the Catholic church and the house fellowship movement. I hope I don't mis-represent their views.

- Much of what is said in many churches is exhortation (sermons) of an acceptable kind. The commands of Christ are, in the main, recognised and taught in many churches. *So shouldn't traditional differences between Christadelphians and other churches be relegated to individual conscience, thereby paving the way for greater cooperation?*

- Much of the teaching in orthodox churches is more open-minded, allowing *individuals* to hold many of the same doctrines as Christadelphians. *So shouldn't Christadelphians adopt a more general statement of faith, one which would allow for greater unity between Christadelphians and other groups?*

All these similarities (should we accept them) pose a problem of difference.[1] If you can't see a *practical* difference, should you insist on a *practical* separation? This question is more poignant if the orthodox church is a 'Biblical' one. The ecumenical challenge is all about what you do about differences.

All churches (orthodox or sectarian) differ somehow in belief or practise. If Christadelphians are like many churches in some of their practises, should they have the same approach to beliefs? Here it has to be recognised that there has been a *revolution* in many churches regarding their beliefs, when we compare them with their earlier predecessors. They are much more varied amongst themselves in the details of their beliefs, and this has come about because they have gradually adopted a more generalist consensus towards Christian doctrine. This agreement upon the more general aspects of Christianity has gone hand in hand with a much more tolerant and open attitude to such doctrines as the kingdom, the nature of man, the devil, the return of Christ, and the atonement at *the grass roots*. (A brief tour of any evangelical Christian bookshop will soon show that there are valuable books on such topics as the promises, the role of Israel, the kingdom of God, and prophecy). This then is the ecumenical challenge to Christadelphianism today - to become less specific on matters of doctrine and more general in the things that are *officially* taught, paving the way for greater cooperation in the community with other churches.

---

[1] The problem of similarities may be the problem posed by a counterfeit. A counterfeit is a virtually indistinguishable copy.

I believe it's a *challenge*, **because truth is at stake**. Times are easy going. It's easy for the importance and value of truth to be forgotten, and it is this **devaluation of truth** that characterizes the ecumenical challenge in its various forms. In the past the heresies were combated concerning the Devil, the Trinity, the Immortality of the Soul, Heaven-going, and others. Today, churches are more pluralistic in their views, more accommodating, more ecumenical. Today, it is not these doctrines that are threatening, but whether making a stand on such doctrines *itself matters*. This phenomenon is a *devaluing* process.

The devaluing process takes various tacks. One hears the following views being expressed among those who question the traditional Christadelphian stance:

i) Christadelphians require ***too many*** doctrines as essential before accepting candidates for baptism. There are only one or two essential Christian beliefs, e.g. that Jesus is God and that he died on the cross for me, and that if I believe and follow him, I shall be saved.

ii) Too much ***detail*** is present in Christadelphian doctrine. We shouldn't specify what is required of believers to the level specified in the *BASF*. The Gospel is meant to be simple, for simple people. Different Christians have different ways of looking at the details, but the simple truths are held in common, therefore we should be united. There are important doctrines, but these are *general* and simple.

iii) Doctrine is important, but can we be ***certain*** that we are right. Isn't it all a matter of interpretation? Equally sincere believers in other Christian groupings believe different things, but their lives are an example to us all. If we can't be certain about doctrinal matters, shouldn't we put doctrine to one side and concentrate on the practical aspects of the Christian faith? After all, we are only human, and we all make mistakes.

iv) The ***relevance*** of doctrine is challenged. If doctrine is not about daily life, its importance is questioned. If doctrine is not as important as was thought in earlier generations, then why is there a separate Christadelphian church? It is quickly affirmed from this kind of devaluation of doctrine that fellowship with other Christians is possible and even desirable. Since fellowship is wholly practical, differences of doctrine, previously thought important, can now be sidelined.

The four tacks are partly logical: there is a complaint about **quantity** (too many), and a complaint about **quality** (too much detail); they are partly psychological: there is a complaint about **certainty** (we shouldn't be so certain), and **sincerity** is put up as the opposite and far better state of mind upon which to insist; and finally, the four tacks are partly **moral**: there is a complaint about the relevance of doctrine to life.

An ecumenical manifesto is, of course, pie in the sky, since none of the orthodox churches are likely to welcome cooperation and unity with the official Christadelphian body as a whole. However, this is not the essential thrust of the ecumenical challenge. The challenge is essentially an *individual* one, because it suggests that *individual* Christadelphians should be allowed to have freer fellowship with other churches. This individual thrust is directed in the following way:

> *Christadelphians may personally believe in the doctrines of the Christadelphian body, and associate with that church. However, because the Gospel is a simple one, there is nothing wrong with individual Christadelphians sharing fellowship with other churches when they so choose. By all means belong to a local ecclesia, but do not let this stop you acknowledging other churches and sharing in their worship.*

Fellowship is a form of behaviour, it involves worship - prayer and singing, it involves exhortation and edification, and many practical works, too many to list. What are the individual consequences if a person participates in fellowship with a variety of local churches?

> *Our views are displayed in our lives and the behavioural choices we make in those lives. We may say that we believe one thing, but our lives may show behaviour of a very different sort. So what does an ecumenical lifestyle say about our real beliefs?*

The first consequence is an acceptance of the ecumenical view, that doctrine is largely a matter of personal opinion, because the Gospel is a general and simple one for all mankind. The second consequence is an acceptance of other churches as a part of the body of Christ, with Christ as their head. This consequence entails an acceptance of the way they induct members into the church, be this through adult baptism, infant sprinkling, or no particular process at all. The third consequence is participation in the worship of a Trinitarian God, both in prayer and in singing. This implies an acknowledgement that such worship is worship in spirit and truth. A fourth consequence is a tolerance of the doctrinal and behavioural norms of other churches in respect of their relationships with the state and the local community - how they practise separation from the world. This may involve implicit acceptance of various kinds of military service, police service, employment in the judiciary, participation in local politics, including the exercise of the vote, as well as good charitable work. It may mean accepting a regime in which there is little control in disciplinary matters. The fifth and last consequence of such behaviour is a rejection of the views and practise of other brethren and sisters in Christadelphian ecclesias.

Ecumenical Arguments
What do we do about these arguments? Let us examine them one by one, and see how they stand up.

1. Too Many Doctrines?
The Bible is a big book, bigger than most books. Most people never read the Bible, instead they get its 'message' in sound bites, and these pass for the Christian faith, but what is the Christian faith? Can we identify the main teachings of that faith? The ecumenical challenge is that the essential Christian faith is general in its content, made up of a small number of basic straightforward doctrines, and wholly practical in its outlook. Details of doctrine are for personal opinions, since establishing them with any certainty is difficult.

We can use various methods to define the Christian faith: a) we can look at the teaching of Jesus, and in particular the summaries of that teaching in the Gospels; b) we can look at the speeches of Acts and see what the apostles preached; c) we can examine the theology of the apostles, taking them as our guide to the teaching of the church; d) we can draw together the repeated themes of the O.T., and so on. This we did in Chapter Two, but what did we achieve in our enquiry?

It is a valuable task to sit and write down what you regard as your statement of faith. It's valuable to reflect on what you regard as important beliefs and what you regard as secondary. However, this exercise needs to be undertaken in an objective way. We need to ask ourselves 'why' we include some things in our statement of faith and exclude others. In this task we are following Paul's advice to 'examine ourselves' to see whether we are in the faith (2 Cor 13:5).

What would a statement of faith include? Our source book is the Bible, so we have to say what we think about the Bible. Our religion concerns God, so we have to say who we think God is - what is his name, his character, and his requirements. We have to say who Jesus was, since he is the centre of the Christian faith. In saying who he was, we have to describe his life - what he did on earth and what he taught. When we explain this, we find ourselves explaining our own condition, that we are mortal, that we need salvation from sin and death. We have to explain that Jesus is the answer to this problem of sin and death, and that his life, death and resurrection are bound up with his answer to our need. Once we have explained his work of salvation and justification, we need to submit to his message, both his moral message and his message of a kingdom, and this involves faith, repentance and baptism. Any mention of the kingdom will bring such topics as the promises to the Jewish fathers, the role of Israel, the place of Jerusalem and our future in that kingdom into a statement of faith. Finally, having set out this faith, we would have to say what would happen to us if we ignored it and put it to one side, and this involves considering the judgement.

Such then are the topics of a statement of faith. It would be difficult to see how we could relegate any of these topics as merely 'optional' or perhaps 'minor' beliefs. The whole idea of options in our central beliefs is not one that can be found in Scripture. In fact, we find the opposite emphasis: there is a 'pattern' to doctrine (Rms 6:17, cf. 1 Tim 1:16, 2 Tim 1:13, Tit 2:7), just as there was a 'pattern' to the tabernacle (Ex 25:40, Acts 7:44, Hebs 8:5). It is the same word in the Greek of Rms 6:17 (translated 'form') and the LXX of Ex 25:40 (translated 'pattern'), which is the word from which we derive the English word 'type'. Paul says we obey from the heart a *form* of doctrine delivered to us, in other words, doctrines had a form or pattern, like the tabernacle (to which Paul alludes). Because they have a pattern, we cannot pull them apart and make them optional. It would be like arguing that the tabernacle could have been made in a variety of ways, and that it wasn't necessary for it to be built in one specific way. Both the tabernacle and the Christian faith have a coherent structure, because each revolves around Christ.

2. Too Much detail?

One of the main challenges to Christadelphians is that they have too much detail in their beliefs: *how is the challenge made up?* Understanding the challenge is crucial these days, because the 'follow up' argument is quickly made that if we have too much detail in our beliefs, then we ought to admit this and allow a wider fellowship with other churches. If we know how the challenge is *made up*, then we can detach ourselves, stand back, and assess its worth.

> *The ecumenical challenge about detail is that Christadelphians have too much detail in their statement of faith. The argument is put that the statement should be reduced and made more general, because the Gospel is a simple one.*

If the content of the Christian faith can be made more *general*, a wider, more ecumenical, fellowship is possible, and the ecumenical approach to doctrine is precisely to generalise its content. Generalisation can be spotted in certain kinds of ecumenical proposals. Here are some examples of how doctrine might be generalised in order to secure an ecumenical objective:

- Trinitarians and Christadelphians could unite if they dropped their particular definitions of Christ and accepted that Christ was God *in some sense*.

- Proponents of the view that the devil is a fallen angel could unite with Christadelphians, if they accept that their view is only *one way of looking at the subject*, and that the devil is *essentially that which is opposed to God*.

- Believers in heaven-going could unite with Christadelphians, if they accepted that there will be an afterlife, but we should *not be specific as to its location*.

- Those who hold orthodox views of the atonement could unite with Christadelphians, if it were agreed that Jesus was the Saviour of mankind, and that his death and resurrection *somehow* made this possible.

These are just examples of generalisation, and each, if accepted, might be part of a hypothetical unity package between Christadelphians and other Christians. *The tactic in each example is to strip away detail to the extent that agreed generalities or communiqués can be achieved between different groups.* Political diplomacy works in a similar way.

This generalising approach is essential to any ecumenical position. Does it match the practise of the apostles? We saw in Chapter Two how the preaching of the apostles was quite detailed, and they expected their audience to respond to their message on their terms. They baptised on the basis of their message. This evidence should control the level of detail in our message, if we want to take our instruction from the Bible.

What about the apostles' teaching, i.e. the teaching that took place after baptism, in the church, to build up the church? Our examples of their teaching come in their letters (cf. Hebs 5:12-6:2). They set out quite detailed explanations of the Christian faith, and when false teaching presented itself to the ecclesia, they opposed the teaching and explained the truth.

What about division and unity? Did the apostles advocate unity and use an ecumenical strategy to achieve that unity? The strategy of stripping away detail from a statement of faith in order to achieve unity is not one that reflects the practise of the apostles. Paul combated division in his letters to Corinth, and positive detailed teaching characterizes his whole approach.

What about God's revelation as a whole? The concepts of Scriptural truth are seldom abstract or general in the ecumenical sense, but rather specific and precise.

3. Too much certainty?

The separateness of the Christadelphian body is based on conviction about the truth,[1] and so the ecumenical challenge attacks this conviction by questioning whether it *should* lead to separateness. Certainty[2] and sincerity are states of mind: we are certain *in our mind* about something, and we are sincere *in our mind* about something. The old joke has one person say to another about their respective beliefs, "You are dogmatic and opinionated in your views, but I am firm and solid in mine". One person's certainty is another's dogmatism. The very word 'dogma' carries bad rhetorical overtones, and it is easy to paint someone in a bad light by announcing that he is 'dogmatic'. In an age of tolerance, many disparage the idea of being certain and firm in one's beliefs, if that means we say *others are wrong*.

The ecumenical challenge focuses instead on sincerity. Equally sincere believers hold different views on the nature of God, Christ, the Devil, or the Kingdom, so surely, the argument goes, having fellowship with them can't be wrong. What is interesting in this position is how certainty, as a state of mind, is *pushed aside* in favour of sincerity. The structure of the argument goes like this:

> *Being certain of your own position is alright, but you can't be certain enough to make a separate stand against other Christian groups, because these may have equally valid views. We should accept this, and allow individuals to exercise their own conscience as to how much contact they have with other churches.*

The doublethink of this kind of argument is breathtaking. A person is allowed to be certain in his own mind,[3] but he is not allowed to press this home, because others *sincerely* hold opposite views, and he can't be

---

[1] The expression "the truth" is a common one in the N.T.; important verses relevant to our theme are 1 Tim 2:4, 3:7, Hebs 10:6.

[2] It's interesting to reflect that *certainty* was the very first virtue to be questioned: the serpent said subtly, 'has God indeed said'. Likewise, it is the modern serpent-like mind that questions whether *we* should be certain of the Word of God.

[3] That is, you are entitled to your own opinions, but you are not entitled to make an issue of them, if others hold different views - so our current culture proposes.

certain therefore of being right!? Putting the doublethink to one side, as a matter of logic, there can't be equally valid contradictory views. *If a view is true, being certain about that view is correct.* If Christadelphian doctrine is true, it follows we can be certain about it, and certain that opposing doctrine is false. Standard logic excludes the concept of *equally valid views* when these are opposing views.

When people insist that sincerity be the most important virtue, they can overlook the fact that sincerity isn't *sufficient* in itself (as a virtue) to enable you to come by the truth. It is only a necessary condition for practising the truth. People can sincerely believe the wrong things, and this is evident from everyday experience. A sincere person does not seek to deceive others, but whether he is deceiving others, isn't just a matter of what *he* intends to do when he preaches.[1] If he preaches falsehoods, then he will deceive others, whether he likes it or not. This is because he is deceived into believing those false things. Sincerity then is not the correct measure for beliefs; it is rather truth and falsity which measures beliefs.

One argument put forward for the ecumenical position is that people are *fallible*, they make mistakes, and thus there is equal probability that any statement of faith will contain errors. Accordingly, it is said that since we may be wrong, we should recognise the validity of the worship of other communities. However, this argues from the general to the particular: it says that as human beings we are fallible, we do make mistakes - this is a general truth; but this doesn't imply that we are wrong in our particular religious beliefs, neither does it imply that we should recognise the *validity* of other Christian worship, if it is not worship of the Father in spirit and in truth (Jn 4:24).

We evaluate true beliefs with evidence and argument. Hence, the Scriptures advocate proof as a tool in our investigation of truth and falsehood:

---

[1] Of course, sincerity may be absent from the motives of some: Paul says of his opponents, '...the one preach Christ of contention, not sincerely...' and '...in pretence...', and contrasts this attitude with preaching Christ '...in truth...' (Phil 1:16-18).

> "Beloved, believe not every spirit, but try the spirits whether they are of God: because many false prophets are gone out into the world."
> 1 Jn 4:1

> "Prove all things, hold fast that which is good..." 1 Thess 5:21

> "Examine yourselves, whether ye be in the faith; prove your own selves. Know ye not your own selves, how that Jesus Christ is in you, except ye be reprobates?" 2 Cor 13:5

> "That ye may approve things that are excellent; that ye may be sincere and without offence till the day of Christ." Phil 1:10

That there would be a need to prove things is part of the design of God. In the Law he had said that he would send false prophets among the people to prove whether they loved Him (Deut 13:3). Hence, there was a need on the part of the people to prove that they did love God by continuing to believe in Him rather than in false gods. This process of proving is a process of discerning and establishing certain things.[1] Once this is done, we can *then* be sincere in what we believe (Phil 1:10).

> "Therefore let us keep the feast...with the unleavened bread of sincerity and truth." 1 Cor 4:8

Moreover, certainty is an attitude that we are commended to have. The problem here is that certainty is often taken for dogmatism, but while the Scriptures don't talk of dogmatism, they do talk of certainty:

> "These all died in faith not having received the promises, but having seen them afar off were assured of them, embraced them, and confessed..." Hebs 10:13

---

[1] See also Acts 1:3, 9:22, 18:4, 19:8, 26.

> "...stand fast in one spirit, with one mind striving together for the faith of the gospel..." Phil 1:27

As we noted in the previous chapter, concepts like *standing fast*, *establishing*, and grounded and *settled* are all used to define our relationship to the Gospel. For these reasons then, we shouldn't jettison certainty as a quality of our faith.

A Brief Excursus on 'the truth'
The phrase, 'the truth', is used widely among Christadelphians. This has been a cause of offence to some onlookers. They argue that it is 'boasting' to claim that you have 'the truth'. This charge is certainly in keeping with the spirit of the age, but from a N.T. perspective, those who were true disciples, part of the N.T. church, possessed the truth, and Paul boasted of this fact. So if Christadelphians stand in Paul's traditions, they can make the same claim.

> *The phrase, 'the truth', seems to be used in a substantive sense, it's not just a collective noun referring to a statement of faith, or particular doctrines, but rather, it has an active role in the life of the believer.*

There is a sense in which the true disciples of Christ are 'of the truth' (Jn 18:37, 1 Jn 3:19). They belong to the truth, and hear the voice of their master. They are sanctified through the truth (Jn 17:9, 2 Thess 2:13). It makes them free (Jn 8:32). They are meant to speak the truth in love building themselves up in Christ (Eph 4:15). They possess the truth; it is 'in them' (1 Jn 1:8, 2:4, 3 Jn v1, v3), and consequently they are allowed to *boast* of this fact along with Paul (2 Cor 11:10).

Indeed, God has chosen his disciples through *belief of the truth* (2 Thess 2:13), and so it is God's will that all men should be saved and come to a *knowledge* of the truth (1 Tim 2:4, 1 Jn 2:21, 2 Jn v1). With this knowledge of the truth, there is no lie associated, and from this belief, there is obedience of the truth (Rms 2:8, Gal 3:1, 5:7, 1 Tim 4:3, Jms 3:15, 1 Jn 1:6, 3 Jn v12), through which the soul is purified (1 Pet 1:22).

This role of 'the truth' runs counter to the ecumenical spirit of our age. In this spirit, truth is not so important as the kind of life you live before God. Ecumenical Christians allow a wide variety of beliefs within their churches. And so it is difficult to see how they can be chosen and sanctified by belief of the truth, if this 'truth' varies from person to person. The church is meant to be the pillar and ground of the truth (1 Tim 3:15), but it is difficult to see this in a church which, say, allows differing views on such doctrines as the nature of Christ and of God, the Holy Spirit, the atonement, the afterlife, the kingdom of God, death, *and so on*.

It is possible to fall from 'the truth',[1] and this truth has its opponents. Peter and Barnabas walked not uprightly when they refused fellowship to Gentiles (Gal 2:14). These apostles had listened to 'false brethren' who went around causing havoc in the church. These false teachers had not learnt the truth as it was in Jesus (Eph 4:21), neither had they a love for the truth (2 Thess 2:10) that they might be saved. So for a brief time, they carried Peter and Barnabas with them. They held the truth in unrighteousness (Rms 1:18), but those who hold the truth in righteousness should walk in a way that shows the truth (2 Cor 4:2).[2]

This concept of falling from the truth, or the idea of there being false brethren, doesn't fit well in more open churches where there are a variety of beliefs. Those destitute of the truth were to be withdrawn (1 Tim 6:5), but those who acknowledged the truth with a repentant spirit were to be received (2 Tim 2:25, Jms 5:19). (Always remembering that wilful sins committed after receiving the knowledge of the truth are not forgiven (Hebs 10:26)). In any event a Christian church should expect there to be false teachers opposing the truth. It was the same for Moses (2 Tim 3:7-8), and it would be the same for the N.T. ecclesias (2 Tim 4:4). It is just as likely today. Why - because God has always desired to test those who claim faith in him with a delusion or a deception. It was so for Adam and Eve. It was the same

---

[1] It is worth observing here that there is a difference between making expositional mistakes about a Biblical text and not being in the truth. A person can hold the truth and be in the truth, understanding what the truth is, but he may still make expositional mistakes about the difficult passages of the Bible.

[2] Doctrine is manifested/typed in behaviour; hence you can *do* the truth.

for the cities of Israel (Deut 13:3). It was the same for the N.T. church (2 Thess 2:11).

What was 'the truth'? Paul defines the truth to be the truth of *the Gospel* (Gal 2:5, 14, Col 1:5). He was a minister of this truth in Christ in all *verity* (1 Tim 2:7, Tit 1:1). The Jews had a form of the truth in the Law, and this was their boast (Rms 2:17-20); so it could be found in the law, if there were 'hearers to hear'. It also predated the Law, being connected to the promises (Rms 15:8), of whom Christ was a minister. These are general specifications of 'the truth'; and an indication of the doctrines to be accepted.

Doctrines make up 'the truth', and so there are doctrines to be rejected. Doctrines such as forbidding marrying and abstention from meats were to be rejected by those who believe and know the truth (1 Tim 4:3). Someone who believed that the resurrection was past already erred from the truth and the faith (2 Tim 2:18). Jewish fables and commandments of men are also contrary to the truth (Tit 1:14).

4. Is Doctrine Relevant to Everyday Life?
It is often heard that doctrine is not relevant to daily life, and for this reason its importance is diminished in some people's minds. The argument is easily made with some doctrines, for example, one might hear the following kind of verbal reply after a doctrine has been explained: '*Yes, but does it really matter whether...*', and thinking of doctrines that have received this reply is easy. The argument has a crucial assumption: that doctrine *has to be about daily life* in order to be worthwhile. Much doctrine **is** relevant to daily life, but the assumption overlooks the fact that doctrine is itself a practical *work* or duty (Jn 6:29, Tit 2:7). In the N.T., it is often made out to be something that we ought to be engaged upon, alongside, for example, the work of looking after widows and orphans (Jms 1:27). Since this work is itself worthwhile, it does not have to have a further impact on our daily life, but often doctrines do have such an impact. It is our duty to consider the Law, its types and patterns, for they teach us about Christ; and our doctrine in this area is a cooperative effort. It is our duty to consider the prophets and explore what they say about the return of Christ, else why are they written? Such considerations may have a direct 'one on one' impact on how we regulate our lives, but the practise of attending to doctrine will also have a more general

effect. The bustle of life can put thinking on the back burner, but Paul counselled Timothy to give attention to reading, exhortation and doctrine (1 Tim 4:13). This is especially the responsibility of leaders in the ecclesia, but their example is also ours (e.g. 1 Tim 4:12).

Our practical life can be regulated by commands, instructions, or advice. For example, a command such as 'Thou shalt not commit murder', has a direct bearing on our practical life. But such a command supplies no reason for not committing murder. If we want to know why we should not commit murder, we have to seek a reason. One kind of reason appeals to authority. It might be said that you should not commit murder because God has so commanded. However, there is another kind of reason, and this is one that God himself supplies for such a command. *This other kind of reason is the doctrine related to the command.*

The role of doctrine is not just to teach some rather abstract truths about God, Jesus, the future kingdom of God and the atonement. The purpose of doctrine is not just to give us some theory to believe and have no effect on our lives. Instead, the point of doctrine is to control our practical life upon the earth. The purpose of doctrine is to give direction and purpose to our lives.

Works are important because they *show* something:

> "Yea, a man may say, Thou hast faith, and I have works: shew me thy faith without thy works, and I will shew thee my faith by my works." Jms 2:10

Relating works to our faith is important; we cannot be saved by our own works, as if they were sufficient to grant us merit in the eyes of God. How then do works relate to doctrines? Let me take two examples (many more could be given). The examples use expressions of inference to make the connection between faith and works, words such as *for, therefore, seeing that*, and so on:

Example 1 - the connection between God's image and violence
Violence is ever present today on television, in the media and on our streets. It is popular in entertainment, but denounced in real life (a curious schizophrenia). What does the Bible say?

> "Whoever sheds man's blood, by man his blood shall be shed; for in the image of God He made man." Gen 9:6

This command, delivered by God, is a good illustration of my point. The instruction is not to commit murder (or violence). But a reason is supplied - *for in the image of God He made man*. If we ask the question: 'Why shouldn't we be violent towards others?', here is the reason - because man is made in the image of God.

Doctrine underpins behaviour. It is a first principle that man is a created being, made in the image of God. This is a piece of theory, if you like to describe things that way. But however we describe it, the plain fact of the matter is this - we must not be violent towards others; because if we are violent, we show that we do not care that (believe that) man is made in the image of God. If we are violent, we are in effect denying this doctrine *in our behaviour*. James makes the same point in his instructions concerning the tongue. If we curse others, what does this show about our belief in the doctrine that man is made after the similitude of God (Jms 3:9)?

Example 2 - connections between redemption and assets
The connection between belief and works can be shown by looking at two cases that illustrate the connection between the doctrine of redemption and how Israelites were meant to handle their assets:

1. In the Law there were laws of release for Hebrew creditors. Here was a form of regulated behaviour - works. The point of this law was to teach a *fact*: God had promised them that they would be lenders to the nations and not vica-versa, and they were to be the rulers of the nations (Deut 15:6).

2. The law of redemption of Hebrew slaves was linked in with facts of history. Just as they had been redeemed from Egypt, so too they were to redeem their Hebrew slaves every seven years. But it's not just some history. Their obedience to this command showed that they believed in their redemption, and that it was the God of Moses that redeemed them (Deut 15:15).

There are many today who say that doctrine is not important. All that matters, they say, is that you believe in Jesus and live a good life.[1] They say that all you need to believe are one or two essential things, and the rest is optional, but this view is deceptive. It lulls you into thinking that doctrine is not important. It suggests that doctrine has nothing to do with our practical life before Christ. Nevertheless, doctrine has everything to do with our practical life. Each doctrine you care to examine[2] (and I have only chosen two examples) is meant to be reflected in various aspects of our life. Our life is meant to *typify* the doctrine we believe, and God has shown in the Scriptures what aspects of our life are meant to manifest the various doctrines that go to make up the truth.

Conclusion

The practical outcome of the ecumenical challenge affects worship, the worship of the community and the worship of other churches. There are three or four types of worship in the Bible:

- The first is true worship, he who worships God *must*[3] worship Him is spirit and in truth (Jn 4:24).

- The second is a worship of the *"know not what"* (Jn 4:22).

- The third is *vain worship*, which characterized the Jewish sects who taught the commandments of men (Matt 15:9).

---

[1] The view that doctrine does not matter can be an example of 'salvation by works'. This can be seen in a sentiment like the following: *the members of church xxxx lead exemplary Christian lives, and the fact that they believe in this or that false doctrine, I am sure, will not be held against them.*

[2] Other doctrines that can be represented in human behaviour include: the order of the creation of man and woman; the relationship of Christ to the church; the Fall; *and so on.*

[3] The *must* here is a necessity. This is often overlooked by those who seek a wider fellowship, since that wider fellowship usually embraces Christians with divergent and contradictory views all worshipping together in the same church.

- The fourth kind of worship is the worship of false gods, (Ps 97:7, Is 2:8).

Three of these kinds of worship concern the God of Israel, while the fourth concerns the idols of the nations. Only one kind of worship of the God of Israel is acceptable, and this is worship in spirit and in truth. The other two kinds of worship directed towards Yahweh are not satisfactory. In one case, Christ said to the Samaritans,

> "Ye worship ye know not what: we know what we worship; for salvation is of the Jews." Jn 4:22

The Samaritans held to the Law of Moses. They used titles of God and forms of address in their language of worship, derived from that part of the Scriptures. They did not accept the writings of the prophets, indeed, they were disparaging of them. Jesus' reason for saying that their worship was a worship of the '*know not what*' was that salvation was of the Jews.[1] This was the doctrine that the Samaritans denied above all others.

The intention of the Samaritans was to worship the Father, this Jesus accepts when he says,

> "...the hour cometh, when ye shall neither in this mountain, nor yet at Jerusalem, worship the Father..." Jn 4:21

But this intention was set aside by Christ. They still worshipped something they did not properly apprehend. This shows that a person's own mental states (like sincerity) in worship are not sufficient to establish true worship; knowledge of the truth is also required.

This is important because much Christian worship in its outward appearance is identical across all Christian churches. A person can be doing the same thing in any number of churches, but this is not enough, although it can *seem enough*. And here lies a possible deception:

---

[1] The claim was that Jacob was *their* father and that they, not the Jews, were the true descendants; their lineage was from Ephraim and Manasseh.

because it can *seem* enough, a person can be misled into thinking that it *is* enough, and that his worship of the Father is acceptable regardless of truth.

Orthodox Christians derive their language of worship from the Scriptures, as well as their own tradition, and this embraces falsehood in the matters of who God is, Jesus and the Holy Spirit. It can be argued then that some orthodox Christian churches 'worship [they] know not *what*', for like the Samaritans they have corrupted the Law and rejected the doctrines of the prophets and the writings.

The worship of the Samaritans was different to that of the Pharisees and other Jewish sects. They were Jews, and Jesus had said that salvation was *of the Jews*. The sects of Judaism agreed with this, and they also held that Samaritans were outside the pale of salvation (not being Jews). Nevertheless, their worship was **vain**. This vanity was entirely due to their enslavement of the people with additional commandments. This implies that what you do, your practical life, is very relevant to your worship. If you add commands to your life you can negate and frustrate the true practise of religion, and make that religion vain. In this case, it is not that the Father is not worshipped, but rather that this is a waste of time unless you correctly apply his requirements to your life.

For some orthodox Christian churches (e.g. Roman Catholics), it can be argued that they have added such commandments. There is the requirement to believe certain creeds; there are various restrictions on priesthood; there are the ritual practises in worship; there are the penances, and so on. In these ways, such commandments frustrate the worship of the Father and make that worship vain.

The danger then in the ecumenical challenge is that it invites participation in various kinds of worship, which for various reasons, are unacceptable to God. In these last days, I don't think we should under-estimate its possible effects.

CHAPTER FOUR

Ecclesial Autonomy and Inter-Ecclesial Relationships

Introduction
In this chapter I want to look at three topics. The first is **ecclesial autonomy**, the second is **inter-ecclesial relationships**, and the third is **guilt by association**. These topics are often raised in fellowship discussions. Some people say they are the *nub* of the issue.

There are several smaller Christadelphian fellowships and one large fellowship. The larger fellowship guards its idea of ecclesial autonomy, whereas the smaller fellowships emphasize the unity of all ecclesias in their fellowship, which is a realizable goal given their size. The smaller fellowships also emphasize the need for purity of fellowship and the possibility of guilt by association, and so they eschew contact with other fellowships.

We should not oppose the idea of ecclesial autonomy, or inter-ecclesial unity, for both ideas have validity: it's just a question of their application - a matter of balance. How should autonomy and unity coexist together in the body of Christ? This is a Gordian knot that we must attempt to cut. We must also consider how to apply the idea of guilt by association. We shall argue that while presently there is no warrant for the idea of guilt by *mere* association being applied to Christadelphian fellowships, association does bring responsibilities, and if we ignore these, then we will be guilty of some failure in our walk.

These are difficult topics about which to write. One reason for this is that I am concerned with principles rather than examples. My concern is not the history of a division or of a particular doctrinal trouble, but herein lies the problem. The principles are often agreed upon, surprisingly, across the fellowships, but the application of the principles varies from ecclesia to ecclesia.

We will be discussing principles in this chapter, and in the next chapter we will be examining specific examples - the so-called 'fellowship passages'.[1] Some of these passages are directly relevant to our discussion of fellowship principles, and so readers ought to read both chapters together in order to gain a more comprehensive picture of Biblical teaching. Readers will perceive a bias towards the O.T. in this chapter, but this will be redressed in the next chapter.

The subject of fellowship is a difficult one. It is not an issue where you can take a detached view and 'agree to differ',[2] but it is an intensely practical subject. It affects your whole life and sense of identity as a Christian. People need a sense of identity and a sense of purpose, and this is often supplied by being a member of a community of fellow-thinkers. When the community begins to fracture, this can be a very unsettling time, because people's confidence in their beliefs is subjected to questioning.

Brethren and sisters, committed to Christ, live their lives in a community and the community is very important.[3] It is made up of their family and friends. Human beings are social animals, and they have a great need for company, and the expression of love that goes with being part of a group. When a fellowship problem rears its head, the love and security that go with being part of a fellowship becomes

---

[1] This chapter is more general, while the next will be more concerned with biblical exposition and the classic 'proof texts' in the doctrine of fellowship.

[2] It is astonishing to find many people who are resigned to letting the divisions persist until the judgement seat.

[3] There is some force in the view that says the current boundaries between the fellowships are wrongly placed. Brethren and Sisters often find more in common with others in different fellowships. For example, perhaps like-minded conservative brethren should be in one fellowship, and like minded liberal brethren in another fellowship. Fellowships *of any reasonable size* tend to have a mixture of each type of person.

threatened, and people become anxious and fearful for themselves and others.

The experience of division can be very damaging to the body of Christ. Some will understand the issues involved, but many others will not grasp the cause of the trouble. Typically, stronger brethren will square up and oppose each other on the cause of the trouble, and those who are weaker and less able to understand are often pulled along in one direction or the other.

Trouble is all the more tragic when its cause is unnecessary, although protagonists will never see it in this way. The qualities of the flesh manifest themselves in a division and add to the tragedy. There is strife, there is hatred, and there is mistrust. The particular vices of the tongue also show themselves. There is rumour, there is gossip and there is backbiting. All too often the need to discuss a matter calmly is overridden by rhetoric and the need to be 'proved right', and so win the flock. Pride is very much to the fore, because protagonists see that their own status is involved in the outcome of the division.[1]

Despite all these negative overtones, separation is inevitable. Jesus prophesied that there would be division (Lk 12:51-53). People are naturally reluctant to participate in division, but such reluctance can lead to worse results in the end. In the apostolic church, the apostle Paul carried out a separation on at least one occasion (Acts 19:9),[2] and in the history of Israel, there are examples of block separation in the congregation. For instance, in response to Solomon's apostasy, the nation was divided *by the angels* to protect the northern tribes from that

---

[1] The qualities of the flesh are effective in persuading people. A rough and ready indicator of where truth lies in a troubled situation is provided if we look for who is manifesting the qualities of the flesh.
[2] This example, often overlooked, shows Paul *making disciples* within the framework of the synagogue and separating the disciples from the Jewish unbelievers. The Jews, disputing with Paul on the things concerning the kingdom, spoke evil of the way and Paul separated the disciples from the synagogue for their own protection. This case of separation is analogous to the separation that Christadelphians maintain from the churches of Christendom. It is *their* view that we lie outside the pale of salvation, and this is an evil speaking of the way.

apostasy (1 Kgs 11:11-13). Or again, *God* reserved (i.e. kept separate and protected) to Himself seven thousand in the days of Elijah.

Separation is necessary when the truth of the Gospel is openly challenged, and the body of Christ needs protecting from those who would take the sheep from the flock. The following question can be put: **what divisions are necessary, and which divisions are manifestations of the fleshly tendency to divide up into sects** (Gal 5:20)? The heart is deceitful above all things (Jer 17:9), so how can we know that we are making the right decision?

Ecclesial Autonomy

What does the expression 'ecclesial autonomy' mean? A working definition would be this:

An ecclesia or fellowship is autonomous if it governs itself.

With smaller fellowships, the fellowship is the only unit of ecclesial life. *It* makes judgements on matters of doctrine and morals as a whole. *It* is the autonomous unit. *It* allows no deviation from the fellowship-wide norms. In a larger fellowship, ecclesial autonomy is more in evidence. As members of a wider fellowship, each ecclesia subscribes to the common statement of faith for the whole fellowship, but there is less inter-ecclesial control of affairs.

Brethren and sisters are on a spectrum. At one end there are those who think that there is no place for the idea of ecclesial autonomy, and at the other end, there are those who guard this autonomy.[1] Problems cluster around either view. If there is too much autonomy, then ecclesias might well start allowing major differences to coexist on matters of first principle doctrine. If there is too much central control over ecclesial matters, this will tend towards fragmentation, as the body finds it increasingly difficult to maintain complete agreement on all matters. It's all a question of practical wisdom.

---

[1] If ecclesial autonomy is coupled with a lack of inter-ecclesial leadership and responsibility, the result can be ecclesias who have a significantly different balance in their message from the mainstream of Christadelphian ecclesias.

The principle of autonomy is seen in the book of Revelation and the letters to the seven city ecclesias. They were clearly in differing degrees of health, with faithful and unfaithful alike in the ecclesia.[1] Each was addressed *in turn* and the majority were counselled to change their ways. At the time of the letters, each was still in the hand of Christ (Rev 1:16, 2:1), despite their many problems, but this was not guaranteed unless they repented.[2]

The Organisation of the Early Churches[3]

All the evidence in the N.T. points to the church being organised around cities, towns and villages. This is not a particularly startling fact, but it's one upon which we can *base* the notion of ecclesial autonomy. Examples of churches include the following:

"the church of the Thessalonians" (1 Thess 1:1, 2 Thess 2:1)
"the church of the Laodiceans" (Col 4:16)
"[the] church" at Philippi (Phil 4:15)
"the church of God at Corinth" (1 Cor 1:2, 10:32, 2 Cor 1:1)
"[the] church" at Jerusalem (Acts 8:1,3, 11:22)
"the church which was at Antioch" (Acts 13:1)
"[the] church" at Caesarea (Acts 18:22)
"the church at Cenchrea" (Rms 16:1)

This structure implies a measure of ecclesial autonomy, since the ecclesia was the main functional unit. This autonomy came about in the following way:

> *In the early church, the ecclesias were subject to apostolic guidance and authority. To cater for the future, elders were appointed in each ecclesia to direct its activities (Acts 14:23, 1*

---

[1] For example, Sardis was an ecclesia which was dead, but there were those who had not defiled their garments in that ecclesia, and who were worthy. They were counselled to strengthen the things that remained (Rev 3:1-5).

[2] In our own day, I am not suggesting here that there are ecclesias in a state like those addressed by Christ. The situation between fellowships is not like that in Asia, since there is a common basis of faith between the fellowships.

[3] This is dealt with in more detail in Chapter Six.

Tim 3:1ff, Tit 1:5ff). This system of elders implies that ecclesias were to decide their own affairs.

The apostles didn't set up a permanent structure of regional councils headed by bishops; neither did they favour international oecumenical councils to determine matters, although, as we shall see, a similar council occurred once (Acts 15). The N.T. mentions regions of churches,[1] but these are regions of city churches, and not regional churches with a fellowship identity.

Discipline of the Ecclesia

Discipline in the ecclesia was both **corrective** and **protective**. Often in treatments of fellowship, this distinction is not recognised. In N.T. terms, a corrective action is corrective of wrong aspects in a person's life, whilst a protective action is protective of the ecclesia. Discipline in an ecclesia was a matter primarily for the elders in that ecclesia. At the same time, it is clear that those with apostolic authority also applied disciplinary measures.[2] The principle that the *elders* of an ecclesia applied ecclesial discipline can legitimately be called **the principle of ecclesial autonomy**.[3]

One of the main qualifications for overseers in the ecclesia was the ability to rule one's own house, and have children in subjection with gravity (1 Tim 3:4). They also had to be able enough to exhort and rebuke the gainsayers (Tit 1:9), holding fast the sure word. They had to restore those overtaken in a fault (Gal 6:1), be apt to teach (1 Tim 3:2), and protect the flock (Acts 20:31). These qualities suggest that they were to be so qualified in order to be able to exercise discipline in the ecclesia. So we find that Paul emphasizes submission by the flock

---

[1] See Acts 9:31, Rms 16:4, 16, 1 Cor 11:16, 22, 16:1, 19, 2 Cor 8:1, Gal 1:2, 22, 1 Thess 2:14, 2 Thess 1:4.

[2] For instance, one of the primary duties of Timothy and Titus was dealing with teachers of non-standard doctrine (1 Tim 6:3ff). To this end, they were to hold fast the faith and be an example (2 Tim 3:4), and correct by sound doctrine (Tit 2:1). Generally speaking, Paul and his associates were to be examples to local congregations (1 Cor 4:16-17, 11:1, 1 Tim 4:12).

[3] I avoid here a definition of ecclesial autonomy in terms of the ecclesia taken as a democratic unit.

towards those who rule over them (1 Cor 16:15-16, 1 Thess 5:12-13, Hebs 13:7,17). He also instructs elders of ecclesias in matters of discipline (e.g. Acts 20:31ff, 1 Thess 5, 2 Thess 3). Timothy and Titus were likewise to instruct local ecclesias (1 Tim 5 and 6, and Titus, *passim*).

The autonomy of local elders is a strong principle, but it is not absolute. On occasion, ecclesial discipline was a matter for the *whole* ecclesia. In 1 Corinthians 5 Paul addresses a moral problem, and he lays down a principle that the judgement of brethren was to take place **within the ecclesia** (1 Cor 5:12-13, 6:4-5). This principle is a strong one, for it would seem that in matters of civil law, even those less esteemed in the church were to judge rather than 'professional' unbelievers. Indeed, whenever Paul is laying down guidelines on procedures to be followed in the church, the presupposition is that such actions are to be carried out by those *within that ecclesia*. We can dub this principle, **the principle of ecclesial jurisdiction** - the ecclesia is an integral whole in matters of judgement. This is our second principle.

With our limited common sense, it might be thought sensible that any question of discipline should fall to those in the immediate local community of Christians. Such a responsibility would be part and parcel of the "one anotherness" required of believers - to admonish one another, care for one another, look on the things of others, submit to one another and confess faults to one another.

The Role of the Apostles
An ecclesia, then, was an integral unit, but even so, no ecclesia is an island. Paul undertook ecclesial discipline himself *at a distance*, and therefore not as part of the *local* community. To understand how this exception could be, perceiving the nature of Paul's relationship to those ecclesias he corrects is important.

In the opening chapters of his first letter to Corinth, Paul is at pains to set out his relationship to them in a clear and forthright manner. The problem seems to have been that there were divisions, envy and strife at Corinth (1 Cor 1:10). These conditions existed because the Corinthians were carnal (1 Cor 3:1-3). Thus Paul exhorts them to be perfectly joined in the same mind and the same judgement (1 Cor

1:11). The contention was centred on the differing worldly wisdom of certain men. These were discriminating between the wisdom of Paul, Apollos, Peter and Christ, creating factions as a result, glorying in these 'differences' and the men who 'symbolized' them (1 Cor 3:17-23).

In countering this situation, Paul sets out his leadership role in relation to the role of other elders. Paul was warning them as their father, who had laid down the foundation of their church. Local leaders were builders upon this foundation, and ought to take care in their building work (1 Cor 3:10-11, 4:14-15, cf. 1 Cor 6:16, 1 Thess 2:11). Paul's retainers were ministers of Christ and co-labourers with him, having the role of adding to his foundational work (1 Cor 3:5ff). It seems therefore that Paul's work as an apostle, in founding churches, gave him authority to exercise correction *besides* the local elders (cf. 2 Cor 1:24, 10:8).[1]

Making Discipline Relevant
The N.T. mentions various disciplinary actions, carried out by leaders in the early church. For example, there were the actions of beseeching, exhortation, warnings, charges, commanding, reproof and rebuke. How did the elders apply these actions? One principle that they followed can be dubbed **the principle of personal relevance**. This is our third principle of fellowship.

When we examine the N.T. cases of discipline, some actions affect individuals, while others are applied to larger groups. Whether the action is being addressed to individuals, or larger numbers, it is made *personally relevant* to those involved. Ecclesial discipline wasn't applied to those it did not affect. It fits the ecclesial perspective of N.T. life. Local elders with local problems had guidelines to follow from the apostles on what actions they should take when addressing problems. Such actions are made directly relevant to local communities.

---

[1] Major Christadelphian divisions have involved leading figures who act in an inter-ecclesial manner. Letters, circulars and visits have been used to administer a view across the whole fellowship. But have such figures 'founded' the ecclesias they approach? Do they tread on another man's foundations (Rms 15:20)?

One of the problems with block withdrawal in the past is that it has been indiscriminate,[1] and therefore it has violated the principle of making ecclesial discipline personally relevant. Most of the protective and corrective actions in the N.T. have regard to the affairs of particular churches. Is it legitimate to apply such actions to ecclesias not involved in a trouble? Here it may be significant that the only substantial example of large scale inter-ecclesial action - Acts 15 - was nevertheless made *relevant* by an apostolic mission taking the letter of decision around the ecclesias.

Inter-Ecclesial Relationships
The first century ecclesias were not isolated and autonomous. There was inter-ecclesial fellowship, and the basis of this fellowship was the common faith.[2] The concept of the body of Christ was both worldwide and local in its application. This is shown in several ways:[3]

- Apostolic letters were reminders of connections beyond the local scene. The salutations and greetings of the letters sometimes link the addressees with all Christians in their province or elsewhere, e.g. not only Corinth, but 'all who invoke the name of our Lord Jesus Christ in every place' (1 Cor 1:2). In Col 4:13, the churches of the Lycus valley are associated, and Laodicea and Colosse are told to share letters (Col 4:16).

- The apostolic visits were part of the inter-connectedness across the N.T. ecclesias. While local groups of believers enjoyed a high level of cohesion and group identity, they were also made aware

---

[1] It's worth observing here that those involved in a trouble have a test *from God*. If they then extend their trouble to other areas, where the trouble does not exist, where perhaps brethren and sisters are working together in harmony, then they act contrary to God. *God may not have sent their trouble to other areas.* Too often we think that we alone run the church, and forget that God is working to build up the church. Too often we think we can create the pure church, not realising that it is through much tribulation that we enter the kingdom.
[2] It seems silly to propose that the body is one, and yet insist that its parts are independent.
[3] On this see Wayne Meeks, *The First Urban Christians*, (New Haven: Yale University Press, 1983), 107-110.

that they belonged to a larger movement. Paul and others worked to inculcate the notion of a universal brotherhood of believers in the Messiah, Jesus. The repeated visits to the local churches by Paul and others all emphasize this inter-relatedness. A good deal of travel was undertaken between ecclesias, and there are hints in the letters that hospitality for travelling brethren was to be expected (1 Tim 3:2, Tit 1:8, 1 Pet 4:9). Here was a most concrete reminder of what it meant to belong to the church of God: that one would be welcome as a brother in Rome, Corinth or Jerusalem.

- Quite a different sort of reminder of a Christian's obligations to others across geographic boundaries is the collection for the poor at Jerusalem, to which Paul devoted a great deal of energy. He was able to mobilize a large effort, with the help of Titus and certain unnamed disciples. They were appointed by the churches to collect money and send it to Jerusalem.

The same inter-ecclesial fellowship is true today. Leading brethren visit and speak across a country, and through this work, a network of contacts is created, which has the benefit of encouraging the believers in all places, and the benefit of meeting and opposing apostasy in the brotherhood when it arises. There are inter-ecclesial committees for preaching, for pastoral work and for youth work; collections are frequently taken for needy brethren overseas, *and so on*. Of course, if there are block divides, this free intercourse is hindered. Brethren with a *prima facia* identical faith are not allowed to speak and exhort across the divide of block fellowships. To be fair, *written* material is shared across fellowships, *tapes and videos* are also shared, and brethren of different fellowships will attend the special efforts, lectures and schools of other fellowships. But the work of exhortation and teaching in the ecclesias is not shared, so the apostolic example is not fully followed. This is seen when visits overseas (e.g. to Africa), to brethren of one fellowship, does not include brethren who are of a different fellowship.[1]

---

[1] It is a serious matter to export division abroad. It is even more serious to refuse succour and aid to the brethren of Christ just because they are in another fellowship. This succour extends to the sharing of the emblems

So there is a universal brotherhood, and there is also a sense of regional fellowship (1 Cor 16:1). Ecclesias in local regions were to be aware of each other, and care for each other in the exchange of letters and visits. It's all a question of local knowledge bringing local responsibilities to the other local ecclesias. A common set of practices across all the ecclesias of Christ is shown by such comments as:

> "And when they had ordained them elders in every church..." Acts 14:23, cf. Tit 1:5-7

> "And so I ordain in all churches..." 1 Cor 7:17

> "But if any man seemeth to be contentious, we have no such custom, neither the churches of God." 1 Cor 11:16

> "As in all churches of the saints, let your women keep silence in the churches..." 1 Cor 14:33-34

Common teaching across the churches is also shown by the dominance of the apostles. The early church "continued in the apostles' doctrine" (Acts 2:42), and the apostles delivered their teaching to their helpers (1 Tim 6:3), who were to pass it down to others.

Reunion Councils

Acts 15 records a model of inter-ecclesial relationships, a model that is often ignored today. A doctrinal dispute had been fermenting, and it came to a head when certain men from the Judean 'circumcision party' taught in Antioch that circumcision was necessary for salvation. Evidently these teachers had been propagating this doctrine in the surrounding regions of Syria and Cilicia, where the first Gentile churches had sprung up (v23). Consequently, the issue at stake was troubling a large region. A big dispute blew up, and the Antioch ecclesia sent Paul and Barnabas to Jerusalem to get a ruling from the Jerusalem church on the matter (vs 1-2).

Members of the sect of the Pharisees (v5), who believed, took up the dispute (cf. Tit 3:10) in Jerusalem. The apostles and elders privately considered the issue (v6), after which Peter addressed the assembly of the Jerusalem church (vs 7,12). Paul, James and Barnabas followed, delivering the agreed views (vs 12-13).

The solution was in part a compromise, because while the doctrine of salvation by grace was upheld, Jewish sensitivities were nevertheless taken into account. A policy declaration was prepared and dispatched to the troubled area, along with Paul, who was commissioned to deliver the message and settle the churches.

This is the only substantial account of inter-ecclesial peacemaking in the New Testament. The spirit of the action is protective insofar as it was designed to settle a controversy started by false teachers. This would then create the right conditions in the church for the spirit of Christ to grow and be nurtured in the ecclesias. There is no specific element of individual correction in the example, but the decision is carried to all affected ecclesias. Notice also that the action is carried out by elders and apostles of the *leading* church. The issue had been taken to one ecclesia, very much in the style that leading ecclesias have been called upon to settle disputes in our own era. The issues settled in our century may not have concerned a doctrine with the same fundamental importance as the doctrine of salvation. Nevertheless, there is a precedent set in Acts 15.[12]

The Law of Cities
In Deuteronomy 13 the laws of apostasy are given for false teachers. Two situations are described: apostasy within the family, and apostasy within cities:

> "If there arise among you a prophet...saying, Let us go after other gods..." Deut 13:1-2

---

[1] Since fellowships share a common statement of faith, there doesn't seem to be a fundamental doctrine at stake as there was in the days of the Jerusalem council.

[2] In the Law concerning *hard judgements* (Deut 17:8-9) there is similar counsel about collective decision making. And the decision made was binding, just as the council of Jerusalem made binding decisions.

> "If thou shalt hear in one of thy cities, which the Lord thy God hath given thee to dwell there, saying...Let us go and serve other gods..." Deut 13:12-13

The apostasy was the serving of other Gods, and so the false teacher, members of the family, and the inhabitants of the city were to be killed. This shows that there is inter-ecclesial fellowship in matters of doctrine. It shows this because Israelites were to look to other cities other then their own, and if they heard of apostasy in those other cities, they were to take action. Our example concerns the doctrine of God and apostasy in the full sense, for the text envisages altars and devoted things (Deut 13:17); but this is not to say that we cannot learn from the example: there was inter-ecclesial responsibility in matters of the basis of faith under the Law of Moses, and we should similarly practise inter-ecclesial responsibility for the faith.

Does this example from the law justify the division between fellowships? It doesn't seem so, and for two reasons: firstly, there doesn't seem to be a sufficient basis in Deut 13 for justifying block division between the fellowships, *if* the various Christadelphian groups share a common statement of faith; and secondly, Deut 13 concerns *cities*, and would be more applicable to city ecclesias, rather than worldwide fellowships. Moreover, were we to apply Deut 13 in our situation of divided fellowships, we would also have to judge that other fellowships were apostate groups.[1]

If city ecclesias today depart from the faith[2] on fundamental matters, then we should 'enquire and make search, and ask diligently; and

---

[1] This is an acid test. It has been well observed that those who remain divided are still eager and willing to read whatever is published by other fellowships, rejoice in their baptisms, their foreign preaching, and so on. If we take what is published by a fellowship as a barometer of that fellowship, then there is much soundness in the fellowships.
[2] It seems to be the case that if apostasy takes hold in an ecclesia as a whole, then the ecclesia becomes known to the brotherhood. A form of dis-fellowship occurs which leaves the door open, but maintains the truth in opposition to the apostasy.

behold, if it be truth, and the thing certain' (Deut 13:14),[12] then the surrounding faithful ecclesias should alert the brotherhood to the danger and have nothing to do with the ecclesia except to combat the apostasy.[3]

Tribal Divisions

The *Law of Cities* does not completely represent the situation today. The various fellowships are more like *tribes* rather than cities. They are tribes of cities that have nothing to do with the other 'tribes'. How do we approach such groupings? Two examples from Israel's early history illustrate group conflict. If we regard Israel as the ecclesia of God in their land, then the tribes are groups based in various regions. They shared a common faith, but apostasy in one tribe had to be eradicated.

- The incident of the 'tribes versus Benjamin' is one example (Jud 20). The men of the Benjaminite city of Gibeah sinned after the manner of Sodom (Jud 19:22ff). Benjamin refused to deliver up Gibeah to the other tribes, and thus allied themselves to the

---

[1] 'To enquire and make certain' is not followed when ecclesias are in separate fellowships, but rather second hand reports and rumours of details feed the desire for *just talking about another fellowship's problems*.

[2] The law of uncertain murder (Deut 21:1-9) involved the local city in an investigation of the murder, and then a sacrifice. Notice this *local ecclesial* focus. The innocent man Jesus was laid at the door of Golgotha's nearest city - Jerusalem.

[3] This has always been recognised. For example, when in America, certain Berean ecclesias re-united with Central ecclesias, the re-union was achieved on the basis of "the Jersey City Resolution" (*The Christadelphian*, Dec, 1952, p. 376). Clause 3 of that resolution reads: "If an ecclesia is known to persist in teaching false doctrines, or to retain in fellowship those who do, other Ecclesias can only avoid being involved by disclaiming fellowship". With the Australian re-union of the fifties, the second clause of the re-union agreement reads, "If it is established that an ecclesia sets itself out by design to preach and propagate at large, false doctrine, then it would become necessary to dissociate from such an ecclesia" ("Unity" booklet, p. 15). And there is an equivalent paragraph in the statement covering the fifties re-union between Suffolk St and Temperance Hall ecclesias.

behaviour of the men of Gibeah. The whole tribe incurred a guilt through their willing association with Gibeah. War followed and the Benjaminites were defeated and subdued.

- A second case-study from Israel's history concerns the tribes who settled east of Jordan. These tribes built an altar, and this action was understood by the western tribes as an act of apostasy (Josh 22:10ff). They proposed war as a means of eradicating the apostasy, but before the battle was engaged, the eastern tribes explained their motives for building the altar - that it was to be a witness to the common faith shared with the western tribes.

These examples illustrate guilt by association, and the need to take action when apostasy emerges among a larger group than a city. They provide a rationale for block division, when there is apostasy among a subgroup of the body. In such a case, there must be investigation to determine the facts, and argument to establish the truth in opposition to the apostasy. Division may be necessary to maintain the truth.

> *If apostasy comparable to these examples emerges in the brotherhood, and a group is affected, then leading brethren would need to investigate the issue and defend the faith against the apostasy. Division may be necessary to eradicate the apostasy from the brotherhood.*[1]

Apostasy was serious because it compromised the holiness of the people of Israel. God had set up a link between doctrine and behaviour in the matter of the Godhead. God was holy and separate, the only true God, and so His people were to manifest this belief by being themselves holy and separate from the nations and their gods.[2]

---

[1] It has to be stressed that such block division is serious, and designed to meet the threat from another block. Most problems in the ecclesial world will not engender such blocks, they will concern individuals, families or a local ecclesia. In these cases, it would be wrong to escalate a trouble into a larger division.

[2] Holiness is usually related to the world. We should be holy and separate from the world, some however argue that we should be holy and separate from other brethren and sisters who share the same faith.

Hence, withdrawal in the Law has to do with apostasy. This requirement is carried over to the N.T. church for Peter points out:

> "But ye are a chosen generation, a royal priesthood, and holy nation, a peculiar people; that ye should show forth the praises of him who hath called you out of darkness into his marvellous light." 1 Pet 2:9, cf. 1 Pet 1:15-16

This separation from the things of the other nations was part of Israel's ethos, and it is part of the ethos of the Christian church. It follows then that there is a requirement for the church to ensure that such holiness is maintained across the nation and the city churches that constitute the nation, and not only in doctrine, but also in matters of practice.

Block Fellowships
Are there any block fellowships in the New Testament? There were serious problems in the N.T. church, which might apparently warrant modern block withdrawal. On the other hand, perhaps the apostles accepted that the norm would be the existence of ecclesias with varying degrees of spiritual health. If there are no block fellowships in the N.T., should we have several now, especially if each fellowship holds to a common statement of faith? This is the challenge! Should the wider Christadelphian brotherhood be split into several competing distinct autonomous fellowships?[1]

The distinct fellowships are *not* the only groupings within the brotherhood today. Within fellowships there are groupings, and some of these amount to distinct fellowships 'within' fellowships. For example, within the largest fellowship there are groups of ecclesias associated with key social events or various magazines. Relationships can be strained between these groupings, even though they exist within the same fellowship. Is this situation any better than the one which sees fellowships as autonomous separate churches? Should groupings be *within* or *without* the church? Which is the *lesser evil*?

---

[1]Have men tried to achieve purity in their fellowships, but cast aside the weak in the faith in order to achieve this end?

The reason for groupings within the body of Christ is that people manifest a different balance of doctrine and practice, and they then naturally associate with others of like mind. Can this natural form of social behaviour be avoided?

In the N.T. there were groups **within** the church. But notice these groups manifested themselves **within** the church and, as far as our evidence is concerned, they were handled *within* the church. There were three types of group:

- groups based around ethnic identities
- groups based around personalities
- groups based around doctrines

The same kinds of group have no doubt emerged in the brotherhood.[1] It is a matter of practical wisdom how groups are handled; it is not enough to lament our imperfection, we have to be positive.

Groups based around ethnic identities
The early church began as a *Jewish* sect, and it then turned outwards to the Gentiles. As a Jewish sect, there was in the Jerusalem church (which was several hundred) a difference between native Jews, and the Jews of the Diaspora. These ethnic groups fell out over welfare provision (Acts 6:1).

The solution to this problem is instructive for us today. The church immediately got together as a whole and appointed seven servants to oversee welfare provision for the Diaspora Jews. The lesson is clear. When there is disagreement between groups in the church, we should get the church together and thrash out a solution to the problem. If we don't do this, then we appear to favour division.

Groups based around personalities
In 1 Corinthians, Paul addresses various groups in the church at Corinth. These groups were based around allegiance to personalities such as Paul, Apollos, Peter and Christ (1 Cor 1:12). Paul's appeal is a

---

[1] Such groupings often go with generations.

simple one based on the Gospel. Were the believers baptised into *Paul*, or was *Paul* crucified for them? No! It was absurd to contemplate dividing the body of Christ based on leaders. What the followers of these leaders thought, we cannot tell. But it seems reasonable to suppose that each leader gave different emphasis to aspects of the truth, and this might have been the basis of the sectarianism.

Leadership is vital to the ecclesia of Christ, but in all things human there is a danger. Leaders can become forceful personalities and lead 'groups'.

Groups based around doctrines
There were also, at times, doctrinal groupings in the early church. This observation is important, and to be expected. Doctrinal troubles will occur within any ecclesia. The pattern of God's dealings with man since Adam has been that He tests him with *subtle* falsehoods. So doctrinal groupings will exist within the church from time to time. It is the duty of the church to meet such groups. Examples of doctrinal groups include the Nicolaitans (Rev 2:6, 15), the Balaamites (Rev 2:14), and Jezebelites (Rev 2:20).

The main doctrinal group was the Jewish counter-reformation. When the Gentiles were first admitted to the church at Caesarea, Peter went up to Jerusalem afterwards to make his report. He was opposed by believers who 'were of the circumcision' (Acts 11:2). These were evidently a party already at work within the church, for Peter addresses them with arguments appropriate to those who were believers[1], but still attached to the Law. They would no doubt have included Jews determined on subverting the new sect,[2] but there were no doubt genuine Christians who venerated the Law.

---

[1] This grouping had a doctrine to propound: 'except ye be circumcised, after the manner of Moses, ye cannot be saved' (Acts 15:1). Such a doctrine was false, and it was addressed at the re-union council of Acts 15.
[2] This is clear from Paul's description of the circumcision group in Gal 2:1-10, which pertains to the period before the first missionary journey (Acts 11:29-30, 12:25). The group developed in power during the first missionary journey, and this prompted the letter to the Galatians.

Things obviously developed with this group, for later on in Antioch, and under their influence, Peter separated himself and the local Jews (including Barnabas) from the faithful Gentiles, because he was afraid of the party of the circumcision (Gal 2:12-13). Paul withstood him to his face on this matter, seeing clearly that the truth of the Gospel had been compromised.[1] But the conflict between the leading apostles led to the council of Jerusalem recorded in Acts 15, where matters were formally resolved.

> *It would seem from these examples that we ought to expect groups within the church, but there doesn't appear to be any warrant for groups sharing the same Gospel going off on their own, because of disagreements on other matters.*

Inter-ecclesial fellowship between ecclesias existed upon the basis of the common faith. Block fellowships don't seem to have arisen, indeed, the evidence of the council of Jerusalem shows that a mass divide between Jew and Gentile Christian was avoided by the taking of immediate action.[2] The N.T. situation is one where we have ecclesias in fellowship on the basis of a common faith, with each ecclesia having various doctrinal problems being addressed by the apostles, and yet in fellowship with one another.[3]

There was an awareness of a universal brotherhood and this was worked out in practical terms in areas of welfare, hospitality and missionary work. The leaders of the church settled doctrinal disputes.

---

[1] Is this separation, which Paul opposed, something we should learn from? Is the separation between the fellowships something we should oppose, like Paul opposed Peter's separation from the Gentiles?

[2] Our two O.T. examples (Josh 22, Jud 20), discussed above, were likewise resolved straightaway.

[3] Some fellowships look at other fellowships and point out doctrinal groupings within the fellowship. That such groupings exist is a matter of concern, but it shows that the fellowship is in a *normal* state. This was the state of the first century church, and the state of Israel. The point to make is that the groupings based around heresies need to be *removed*.

Ecclesial discipline and withdrawal were carried out at the local level. This is what inter-ecclesial fellowship was in the first century.

Inter-Ecclesial Relations and Guilt by Association

Guilt is incurred when we break commands to which we are responsible. If there are such commands in the Bible concerning association, and these commands are broken, then guilt must follow. There are various kinds of association affecting us and different commands relate to these kinds of association. Accordingly, we can be guilty of various kinds of association. It's that simple. It's important to realise this, because it's wrong to assume that 'guilt by association' is a *singular* idea. Too many people assume it's an idea that is either right or wrong. This is far too simple an approach, and establishing this fact is one of our main tasks.[1]

In fellowship discussions, people talk of 'guilt by association' and by this they often mean 'guilt by *mere* association' or 'guilt by *formal* association', and the *formal* association they refer to is usually **another** Christadelphian fellowship. Does the Bible talk of formal association, and if it does, can you incur guilt by such an association? Here we will see that the Bible verses used to 'prove' *guilt by mere formal association* are usually about *other* forms of guilt by association. Consequently, any antipathy towards other Christadelphian fellowships tends to be based on expositional mistakes.[2] The view that you are guilty by *just being a member* of a main Christadelphian fellowship doesn't hold water.

Perhaps the most fundamental mistake people make in this area is to misapply their data (i.e. the Bible). The question to ask first is: what entity are we talking *about*? If it is another *fellowship* - a global group, then what can we say about it - as a whole? There are many associations **in** a fellowship, some bad, most good, and there will be possibilities of incurring various kinds of guilt by association *within* a fellowship. The same is true of our own fellowship. But if a person avoids such associations **within** a fellowship, then necessarily he

---

[1] We shouldn't be afraid of the expression 'guilt by association'. All we have to do is carefully define its scope and limits.
[2] These expositional mistakes, for the N.T., will be explored in the next chapter.

does not incur any guilt by *such* associations.[1] The same is true of us in our own fellowship. But can we be guilty of something by *just being part* of a formal association like a Christadelphian fellowship?[2]

If we admit that there *are* various associations **in** a fellowship, can we think of a *whole* fellowship *as an association*? I think we can, if we define what we mean by the 'fellowship'. The fellowship is made up of ecclesias and individuals across the world. Most ecclesias and individuals will only have practical dealings with those in a local area. But even so, they are part of a worldwide fellowship. How can this be the case, if they have nothing to do with 90%, say, of the fellowship? The obvious answer is that **a fellowship is formally defined by its basis**. People participate in a fellowship on a formal basis. It follows therefore that this formal definition is the *only* area where we can bear *guilt by formal association*. It's perhaps obvious, once stated.

A formal association has a formal basis, and if this basis is flawed and contrary to the ways of God, then we would incur guilt if we partook of that formal association. So if we criticize another fellowship, and speak of the fellowship as a whole, we ought to speak of its formal basis and criticize it at this level.[3] Here the astonishing fact is that various Christadelphian fellowships share an identical statement of faith. They share the same formal basis. If this is the case, it would seem that a member of one fellowship cannot accuse someone in another fellowship of incurring guilt just by virtue of his membership of that fellowship.

---

[1] Elijah is a case in point. He was *part of* the nation of Israel, but he did not participate in the apostasy of the nation in any way. He was one of seven thousand who were part of a formal association (grounded in the statement of faith - the covenant), but who nevertheless did not associate with the apostate goings-on in the nation.

[2] Christadelphians of all fellowships are formally associated in at least one way, because they all claim the name 'Christadelphian'.

[3] We can, of course, analyse the internal workings of a fellowship and say this or that ecclesia is wayward, or that this or that individual is a false teacher or immoral, but problems will always exist in a fellowship. It was so in the first century. It is a category mistake to see the problems **in a fellowship** and then criticize the fellowship *as a whole*, because a fellowship will also have much good in its midst.

If we take the largest Christadelphian fellowship, its basis of faith is set out in *BASF*. We argued in chapter Two that this statement of faith was a good statement of the Gospel. Can a person incur guilt, by formally associating with ecclesias and individuals that subscribe to this statement? Obviously not, if it represents the Abrahamic Gospel! And if it does *not* represent the Gospel, then a person *can* incur guilt by supporting such a statement. Smaller fellowships have usually added to this statement of faith. Perhaps, then, there is scope for criticism of unnecessary additions to the common Christadelphian statement of faith, since these can devalue the importance and role of the Gospel as the *sole* basis of faith. If they are unsound additions, then the formal basis is flawed, and guilt by formal association can be incurred.

Our main objective is to pin down 'guilt by association' in a Scriptural framework, but we will have to be careful in the points we draw out from the text.

Preliminary Distinctions
Is the principle of 'guilt by association' a clearly defined idea? What do people mean by this slogan? Where should we start in tackling this topic? Perhaps the first questions to ask are these:

- **what or who shouldn't associate with what or whom?**

- **what is the nature of the association that is wrong?**

These are fundamental distinctions, and they can easily get blurred. Let's pose some possibilities:

the what and the whom

- we could talk of **individuals** - Christians shouldn't associate with other individual Christians in certain circumstances.

- we could talk of **groups** - ecclesias or individuals shouldn't associate with other groups in certain situations.

- we could talk of **behaviour patterns** in a person's life, e.g. drunkards should not be associated with, adulterers, and so on. Here we can include **attitudes**[1] that summarise behaviour patterns, for instance, we might say, 'avoid certain attitudes, like *tolerating* wrong doctrine'.[2]

- we could talk of **a particular piece of behaviour** in isolation, e.g. a dodgy deal should not be associated with, or an act of adultery, the teaching of false things, and so on.

A caution is necessary here when we criticize groups:

In order to criticize groups, we have to talk the language of 'groups', and become more abstract in our approach. We must start talking of the state of the group as a whole, thus ignoring distinctions and differences between individuals and ecclesias in that worldwide group. For example, we might say that such and such a fellowship is in a pretty poor state, or that there is the presence of falsehood in that fellowship, and so on. This kind of talk can get quite abstract, for example, groups can be characterized as 'weak' on fellowship, 'self-righteous' about divorce and remarriage, 'dogmatic' on doctrine, 'tolerant' of false doctrine. Such talk allows us to think in block terms and pigeonhole whole groups, dismissing them as we go our way. But how Christ-like (cf. Matt 23) is such talk?

Let us turn from the 'what and the whom' to the kinds of association that might be wrong:

the kind of association that is wrong

- we could say that **the formal association** is wrong, i.e. the formal basis of the association is wrong. However, if the common Christadelphian basis of faith is sound, you cannot be guilty by a *mere* formal association on that basis. If it is unsound, then we do

---

[1] An act is an act, but toleration is a mental *attitude* (manifested in action); and the presence of falsehood is usually the *state* of a group.

[2] This kind of judgement can be sweeping in its scope, and we need to be careful of the tendency man to make dismissive judgments.

bear a certain responsibility, though the framework for such guilt is absent from its terms.

Are you guilty by being 'formally associated' with behaviour that is wrong, or with people in the wrong, when you have no personal relationships with the parties involved? It seems that mere formal association is not enough to incur guilt. There also has to be a framework of working responsibilities for guilt by association to be possible.

- we might say that *various kinds* of **informal association** are wrong, perhaps a private gathering in a home, or having a personal relationship with what is wrong or those in the wrong. Here though it is important to define what we understand by the 'association'. You relate to people in various ways, with various kinds of behaviour. Which are wrong? Are some still allowed? For example, can we still associate with members of our natural family, but refuse to associate with them ecclesially?

How do these distinctions work out in practice? Clearly some associations bring guilt, but do all associations bring guilt? In particular, does formal association in a Christadelphian fellowship bring guilt? How do we correctly apply the Bible, so that we can identify what associations are wrong?

Interpreting the Bible
When applying the Bible in our lives, we make value-judgements. When we extract principles from the Bible, we compare the Bible with our own lives. We 'see' certain analogies between the Biblical situation and our own circumstances, and in this process of 'seeing' we strip away aspects of the Bible story that don't fit our own situation. In this process, we often say that the Bible story illustrates a principle. But it is easy to make mistakes. Two examples, one from each Testament:[1]

Example 1 - Associating with the World
In Genesis 18 and 19 God talks with Abraham about Lot, and we learn the principle that God does not slay the righteous with the

---

[1] Other examples will be given in the next chapter.

wicked (Gen 18:23-25, cf. Ezek 9). The story shows that it is possible for a man to be righteous, and yet associate closely with men of the world. This mirrors the experience of other O.T. patriarchs, for they lived in the world and associated with those of the world. Indeed, today, our souls are vexed at the wickedness of men.

In a certain sense, Lot shows that we are not guilty of sin by associating with the world; we are after all in the world. It would, however, be a misuse of the example of Lot to argue that we cannot be *guilty of any kind of association at all*. We cannot 'extract' a universal principle. If someone does do this, he plainly ignores that detail of the story, which sees Lot associated with the *world*.

It is obvious that Christian association is different from association with the world. Guilt is not incurred by associating with the world in our daily work, but this does not mean that guilt is not incurred by actively involving yourself with some Christians who manifest (in clearly specified ways) the thinking and behaviour of the world. To say this based on the example of Lot would be to ignore the disanalogy that exists between Christian association and worldly association.

Example 2 - Associating with False Teachers
In 2 John we read of itinerant false teachers who *had gone out into the world* (v7, Gk), and who taught a different 'doctrine of Christ'. This was teaching *about* Christ, rather than Christ's own teachings.[1] They

---

[1] This conclusion is based on the following observations: (a) John has just been concerned with what we should believe *about* Christ (v7), rather than his general teachings; (b) John is talking about two groups: the many deceivers who have gone *out* (Gk) into the world with a false view about Christ (v7), and who no doubt have competing false churches associated with them; and, those still in the ecclesia to whom he was writing (v8). It is the first group who are *from the world* who come to the true ecclesias and who should not be received (v10); (c) Those who don't abide in the doctrine of Christ do not *have* God, though they no doubt use much of the same religious language. In John's epistles, this language is used of those who deny Jesus *is* the Christ. A person denying that Jesus is the Christ does not *have* the Father (1 Jn 2:22-23, cf. 1 Jn 5:10-13).

were not to be received (v10), on pain of partaking of their evil deeds (vs 10-11). What does 2 John tell us about guilt by association? It tells us that those ecclesias who receive false teachers *of the world* share their evil. This is something that shouldn't be done. It is a command about association. Disobeying it leads to guilt. What this sharing of their evil works would have been is not specified, but it is likely that it would have involved the normal hospitality and facilities shown to visiting teachers (cf. 3 Jn vs 5-8).

What does John *not* tell us about guilt by association? It doesn't tell us anything about guilt by *mere* association or *formal* association. The sort of association that goes with bearing the name 'Christadelphian', or by being part of a global (collective) fellowship in which there are problems.[12] In 2 John we have a local *ecclesial* situation; John isn't addressing the *worldwide church fellowship*.

How do we apply it today? We ought to apply it in those ecclesial situations that relate to false teachers outside the church who contradict first principle doctrines. We are guilty of wrongful association if we don't follow John's command. If we do apply the counsel of John, our decision is a serious matter, for it carries with it the implication that those whom we do not receive, are **not** part of the body of Christ, but *out in the world*. This was the implication for John, and it must be ours as well. But is John's command applicable to globally divided Christadelphian fellowships? Are some Christadelphian fellowships *of the world*? With these thoughts let us move on to examine the question of formal associations.

Formal and Informal Associations
The Law of Moses represents the basis of the formal association that we know as *Israel*. So let's look at Israel and try and think of Israel as a 'church' - an ecclesia (Acts 7:38). What do we learn? Can Christadelphian fellowships justify separation from other fellowships by referring to Israel? Perhaps the first point to make here is that Israel

---

[1] The apostle John was himself *part* of a fellowship with tremendous problems.
[2] Can a fellowship be pure? Perhaps it can if it's very small. But as soon as it grows, purity decreases. It's a bit like thermodynamics; entropy seems to increase over time.

remained a *unit under the hand of God* until Solomon. Israel's basis of association is expressed thus:

> "Now therefore, if ye will obey my voice indeed, and keep my covenant, then ye shall be a peculiar treasure unto me above all people: for all the earth is mine. And ye shall be a kingdom of priests, and an holy nation" Exod 19:5-6a, cf. Ex 23:23, 32-33, 34:11-14

The basis of the association was the Law and this enshrined the Mosaic covenant. The Law had many laws about associations, and the ordinary Israelite could incur guilt by association if he contravened these 'association' laws. No doubt many Israelites did disobey the Law in these matters, but those who were faithful did not thereby become guilty by association, just because **they were part of the same nation** as those who were disobedient. If we can *see* this, we must also *see* how we can be part of a new Israel, and yet not be guilty through *that* formal association. (If, that is, the formal basis of the association is sound). If we fail to see this point, we may well end up misapplying the O.T. data on fellowship. Such misapplication can lead to wrecking the spiritual nation. I will identify three kinds of disassociation, and indicate where I think they can be applied to day.

(1) Ritual Disassociation
Individual disassociation was required in certain ritual aspects of the Law. For example,

- we find abstinence and avoidance in the laws relating to unclean and clean beasts, fowl, creeping things, and meats (Lev 11:43-47, 20:24-25). God 'called' these things unclean, and their refusal to partake of them was to show that God was holy. It was to be a case of their behaviour showing a first principle doctrine.

- disassociation is prominent in the laws about issues of the body, the plague of leprosy, and the birth of children. This is motivated by a need to maintain the sanctity of the tabernacle (Lev 12:2ff, 13:45-46, 14:33ff, 15:2ff, 31).

These are examples of commands to disassociate from certain behaviour (eating various things), and from certain kinds of people (lepers, new mothers and those with minor and serious issues). They show the need for personal purity and holiness among people **within a nation**, and they do not require people to separate from the nation. They require people to keep away from those *in* their nation who are affected. Notice here that disassociation was handled in two ways: on the one hand some classes of person went out of the camp, (away from their camps, see Num 5:2-3); but on the other hand, some remained in the camp in isolation. In both cases, the individuals were regarded as **part of the nation**, and clearly the Law recognised that some uncleanness did *not* require exclusion from the congregation.[1]

What are the lessons for us today? The uncleanness of the human body in certain conditions is typical of man's *proneness to sin* rather than any particular form of behaviour. Some would hesitate to apply the Law to the Christian church, but if we do extract lessons from the Law, I would suggest that these examples show the following,

- we must refuse to partake of 'unclean things'

- we must keep away from those *in the camp* who are 'unclean'

- we must place outside the camp the more serious cases of 'uncleanness'

From these abstract aphorisms, we cannot infer anything specific about applying the lessons to real behavioural problems. We need to apply them as we are best able, using the particular examples of disfellowship provided in the Bible. Thinking in strictly O.T. terms, brethren will disagree on what to do about uncleanness. All should agree that some uncleanness requires placement outside the camp. But for some cases, some will say that while the uncleanness is to be avoided, those who are unclean can be kept within the camp. The Law recognised differences in the treatment of uncleanness, and perhaps there is wisdom for us in this recognition. For in the body,

---

[1] If we closely compare Lev 15 with Num 5, it would appear that those issues which were of undetermined length required placement outside the camp, while minor issues were handled within the camp, in similar vein to the uncleanness of childbirth.

only some will disobey in a way that requires the action of avoidance.[1] However, in placing people 'without the camp', the faithful make a mistake in their application of Scripture, if they place *themselves* outside the body, *instead of addressing the 'unclean'*. This is an easy mistake to make: we can see that the O.T. teaches 'putting outside the camp' for those who are unclean, but we can end up instead putting ourselves outside the camp along with others that we can influence to our point of view.

(2) Disassociation from Apostasy
The nation *as a whole* could be guilty by association with apostasy. Faithfulness in worship (Ex 23:23-24, 32-33, 34:14-15), and faithfulness to God's moral standards, is linked to the need to remain separate from the nations. If the nation compromised these things, they became guilty as a whole, and the offending *group* in the nation had to be expunged.

- everyone joined to Baal-Peor was to be killed by the judges. But apart from this, a plague was inflicted upon the twelve tribes (Num 25:1-5). The description here, and the refrain of later references (e.g. Ps 106), is that Israel sinned in the matter of Baal-Peor, but it is apparent that only a section of the nation joined themselves to Moab (Num 25:5, Deut 4:3-4).

- the incident of the Golden Calf was an Egyptian apostasy, and those who were not on the Lord's side were slain, but besides this, a plague was sent upon the nation (Ex 32:26-28,35, cf. Lev 20:2-5 (N.E.B.), and Rev 2:16,22-25).

- we see in the *Story of the Second Altar* an example of the whole of Israel making moves to expunge suspected false worship from among them: Phinehas, a priest responsible for administering the Law, recognising Israel's collective responsibility concerning false worship, pleads with the tribes responsible for the Altar to cease their action.

---

[1] In the camp, we must stay away from the tents of some (Num 16:26).

It is clear, then, from the Pentateuch, that Israel were to disassociate themselves completely from the nations (Deut 7:1-7, 20:16-18 cf. 2 Chron 22:7), and it is evident that the Law of Moses was also framed to reinforce proper religion and morals in distinction to Canaanite practice. The application of this today relates to our separation from the world, and the apostate churches of the world (cf. Rev 18:4).

(3) Disassociation from Worldly Behaviour
There is another kind of guilt by association in the Law. This is the kind of guilt that comes from copying the practices of the nations:

> "After the doings of the land of Egypt, wherein ye dwelt, shall ye not do: and after the doings of the land of Canaan, whither I bring you, shall ye not do: neither shall ye walk in their ordinances. Ye shall do my judgements, and keep my ordinances, to walk therein: I am the Lord your God...For whosoever shall commit any of these abominations, even the souls that commit them shall be cut off from among the people" Lev 18:3-4, 29, cf. Lev 20:22-24

Those who committed these sins were to be "cut off" or put to death (Lev 20:3-5). The sins included, for instance, false worship (Lev 20:1-6, 27, Deut 17:2-7), profanation (Lev 17:3-14, Deut 18:9-12) and sexual immorality (Lev 18, 20:7-21).[1]

An Israelite would be guilty if he associated with those who did such things. But the association here that brings guilt is a ***participation*** in such things. An Israelite is not guilty of such things, just because he is an Israelite and others are doing these things. This shows that there is a need to be careful about our associations *within* the body, we should avoid participation in worldly behaviour brought in from outside by those who have faltered in their faith.

Associations in the New Testament
If this is a fair summary of the notion of "guilt by association", as applied to Israel, how do we make the application to the ecclesias of

---

[1] I also would include here behaviour that is not particularly Egyptian or Canaanite, such as loose living (cf. Deut 20:21).

Christ? We have stated already that association with the world is an inevitable fact, but clearly the Law shows that one is not to associate with the world in its practices (cf. 1 Cor 5:9-10). The precedent of the Law shows that **within** the ecclesia there may be various sins of association, but since we are not under the provisions of the law, we would have to look at the N.T. to identify what these sins are today. We have also seen that the nation as a whole could be collectively guilty if it fell into apostasy. But does this apply today? If we apply this warning today, it would apply to circumstances where Christadelphian fellowships abandon their historic faith in favour of the thinking and practices of those around them. But have whole fellowships 'gone over' to apostasy? The commands about disassociation in the N.T. can be succinctly summarised:

- don't associate with bone-idle loafers who are busybodies (2 Thess 3:6,11,14)

- don't associate with bad behaviour, for bad morals leaven the ecclesia (1 Cor 5:2,6-7,11,13)[1]

- don't associate with those who personally trespass against you (Matt 18:15-17)

- don't associate with false teachers who come to your ecclesia (Tit 1:10-11, 2 Jn v10-11)[2]

- don't associate with those who cause schism and splinter groups in the church (Rms 16:17-18, Tit 3:10)[3]

---

[1] Notice that this case is about immoral behaviour. Paul isn't here talking about false teachers or those who hold false ideas about certain doctrines. It's too easy to conflate all these texts and impoverish our understanding of fellowship.

[2] Notice the strength of the language about false teachers - they are *pernicious*, they cause the way of truth to be *slandered*, they are *damnable* and *swiftly destroyed* (2 Pet 2:1-2). Are such adjectives applicable to Christadelphian fellowships?

[3] The 'heretic' to be rejected after the first and second admonition is not a teacher of false doctrine as per its modern meaning, but in the

- don't associate with false teachers in the ecclesia, those who are proud, doting over questions and words, and who refuse correction (1 Tim 6:3-5) [12]

What about those who *don't* disassociate with such things? They become guilty by their association. But their association is not a *formal* association, it is an *involving* [3] association (cf. 1 Tim 5:22). They would be giving hospitality to false teachers, they would be 'going around' with those who were causing schism, they would be 'hanging around' with the bone-idle on street corners, and they would be condoning bad behaviour.

Responsibility and Guilt

The notion of responsibility is important in an analysis of "guilt by association". Law brings responsibilities and the possibility of guilt. Under the Law there are two types of responsibility: **collective responsibility** and **individual obligations**. The basis of Israel's collective responsibility to God was their collective agreement to enter the covenant. From this Law there also flowed their individual obligations.

Collective Responsibility

God dealt with Israel as a whole, because they were made collectively responsible for their affairs, and they could be treated in a collective manner.[4] God punished the nation as a whole, even though the deeds

---

N.T. the 'heretic' is a one who causes division. No doubt, *some* heretics promoted false teaching (e.g. 2 Pet 2:1-2).

[1] Notice the description of the false teacher, Paul does not have in mind those who go astray on points of doctrine but remain *teachable*.

[2] Some mis-interpret this command. It does not mean that at the first sign of wolves in the flock, the shepherds should say, 'There's a wolf over there, let's grab what sheep we can, and get out of this field'.

[3] Sardis is a case in point. Here there were those who not defiled their garments even though they were formally part of an ecclesia with grave problems. They had not incurred guilt by association in the ecclesia, even though the danger of doing so was very real.

[4] Consider, for instance, the function of the Day of the Atonement and its national significance.

done, were perpetrated by individuals. This kind of collective responsibility brings a kind of 'collective guilt', but this doesn't translate into 'everyone is equally guilty',[1] neither does it imply equal responsibility.

> *The righteous in the nation suffer the consequences of God's punishment along with the wicked, because God is treating the nation; but they themselves are not personally guilty.*

If we examine the Pentateuch, we find that the delivery of the Law often presupposes collective responsibility on the part of the nation. This is most apparent when God addresses Israel as a collective entity. For example, in prophetic warnings such as the cursings and blessings (Deut 28, cf. Lev 26, Deut 6 and 7). Or again, in instructions about their duties under the national covenant (e.g. Ex 19:5-6, 23:20-22, Lev 20:22-24).

The system of appointed judges and rulers (set up by Moses, Ex 18:21ff, Deut 1) indicates an awareness of a collective responsibility to see that the Law was upheld. National crises, which resulted from unfaithfulness in some, showed this awareness of collective responsibility before God to obey the terms of the covenant. We have looked at the cases of *Baal-Peor* and the *Golden Calf*. The language used there by God bespeaks a sense that Israel is collectively at fault. Accordingly, while the offenders are dealt with by execution, an additional plague is sent upon Israel by God.

A further example is the sin of Achan in Joshua 7. The description that the Spirit gives of that offence is twofold:

> "Israel hath sinned, and they have also transgressed
> my covenant which I commanded them: for they have

---

[1] Guilt by formal association is like the doctrine of original sin. This says that each individual is personally guilty of Adam's sin by virtue of being associated with him as his descendant. The truth of the matter however is that individuals bear the *consequences* of Adam's sin while not being individually guilty of his sin. And so it was with Israel: they bore the consequences of God's punishments as a group, even though many would have been innocent of the transgression.

taken of the accursed thing, and have also stolen, and dissembled also, and they have put it even among their own stuff." Josh 7:11, cf. 6:17-18

"And it shall be, that he that is taken with the accursed thing shall be burnt with fire, he and all that he hath: because he hath transgressed the covenant of the Lord, and because he hath wrought folly in Israel." Josh 7:15

Achan is the 'classic' passage in 'guilt by association' discussion. Achan had taken of the 'devoted thing', and consequently Israel had been troubled by failure to conquer Ai (Josh 7:2-10). His case illustrates the main point we have to bear in mind:

Collective accountability does not imply equal guilt for all of Israel

One man is held responsible for the sin, with his family (who were regarded as *his*, and who would have known about the deed), and all of Israel suffered the consequences (the 'trouble') of the sin of Achan. They were not equally guilty with Achan at the individual level. Joshua was told, 'Get thee up, wherefore liest thou thus upon thy face?' (Josh 7:10). He was not personally guilty, but the nation as a whole was accountable for the accursed thing in their midst. And so at this crucial stage in their conquest of the land, Joshua and the angel of the Lord removed Achan and his family from Israel.

This kind of 'guilt by association' (collective guilt) is not like the guilt that falls upon those who individually associate with certain kinds of bad behaviour, and who individually associate with particular kinds of people. It's easy to ignore the differences[1] that we have in the O.T.

---

[1] We have said that 'guilt by association' is not a single idea, and collective guilt is a *kind of* guilt by association. It's a category mistake to lump O.T. and N.T. examples together and pronounce: 'Look! guilt by association is taught in the Bible', or 'Look! collective responsibility is a Bible principle'. We need to appreciate the variety in God's teaching.

concerning the various kinds of guilt by association and thereby misjudge fellowship questions.

For collective guilt to be applicable to a group there needs to be a collective basis of responsibility. The responsibility needs to be taken on collectively and maintained collectively. Israel was a nation who collectively entered a covenant with God. Further, collective guilt needs to be addressed *by those able* to engage the collective group. *God* was able to address the whole of Israel, and he did so - he punished them as a whole. National leaders, like Moses, were able to address the whole nation, and they were able to execute policies that affected the nation.

When we think of this type of *corporate view* presented in the O.T., we naturally ask: Is the church a corporate entity collectively responsible before God for its affairs? If this is the case, it would need its 'priests and Levites', its 'tribal princes', its 'prophets' and its 'leaders'.[12]

There are then some important differences between Israel and the church, which we need to take into account when thinking of this kind of guilt by association:

- Israel was governed by a hierarchy of rulers, who were appointed by Moses. There was a tribal structure, through which discipline was applied. The church, though, was organised into ecclesias, and discipline was given to local elders. There was no national (or international) leadership set over the church. The apostles did not choose to follow the structure of Israel in the wilderness, but rather the synagogue model of the exile.

- In a time of national crisis, the *whole* of Israel is pictured as responsible for a transgression of the law. Large numbers were often involved. In these circumstances we see *God addressing* the nation taking the initiative and administering the necessary

---

[1] But unlike Israel, brethren do not 'command' a tightly knit group like a nation. They are not in dialogue with God and working with him to implement His will. Consequently, their accountability is different to that of the priests, prophets and leaders of Israel.

[2] Some orthodox churches have structures like that of Israel.

discipline. The nation's leaders, its priest and prophets were involved in this action *of God*. But the church isn't in this kind of situation today.

- The old covenant was a *national* covenant, whereas the New Covenant is one entered voluntarily by individuals. Israel was a 'theocratic' state, and its political and religious aspects were bound together. Today this is not so - the 'church' is a 'free' society, composed of those who voluntarily unite together - their only bond being mutually shared convictions.

The church is not like Israel in these respects. Its ties are looser, it lacks spirit-guided leadership, it lacks a national structure, it is international in breadth, and so on. Because of these differences, Israel's collective responsibility was translated by the apostles into an *inter-ecclesial responsibility of leaders*.[1] Ecclesial leaders have a responsibility to each other in respect of maintaining the faith.

To summarize:

- **Collective responsibility does not imply equal responsibility.** Brethren and sisters are given different roles in the church, and they work in different localities. Some brethren rise to positions of inter-ecclesial leadership and take on *these* responsibilities. But not all are leaders. There is no justification in the Israelite example of collective responsibility, for each brother or sister being made to feel responsible for matters outside their sphere in the truth.

- **Israelite collective responsibility was not carried over into the N.T. period by the apostles.** Instead, they practised *inter-ecclesial responsibility of leaders*. Ecclesias and leaders can neglect their inter-ecclesial duty if they break away from the body to form separate fellowships.

In all this, Christadelphians have to have a clear sense of the separation of their calling. They have to firmly grasp the need to remain

---

[1] Supplemented by each ecclesia's own responsibility for its faithfulness (look at Rev 2, 3).

separate from the world, its associations, and its religions (2 Cor 6:14).

Individual Responsibility and the Prophets
This principle is self-evident everywhere in the Bible. With regard to the Law those details of the sin-offerings particularly demonstrate the principle (e.g. Num 5). In looking for a one verse quote, Ezekiel 18 is perhaps the clearest example:

> "As I live, says the Lord God...the soul that sins it shall die" Ezek 18:4

It is a fundamental principle that God judges each according to his works. Even so, such a principle is not absolute. Saints of old 'took on' the sins of the people. (For example, Ezra's prayer in Ezra 9, particularly v6ff; Nehemiah's prayer in Nehemiah 1, particularly v6ff; Daniel's prayer in Daniel 9; Jeremiah's prayers, for example see Jer 3:25, cf. Ps 106:6). Their prayers *took on* the guilt of the nation, identifying themselves as part of their nation, accountable to God. They did not eschew their nation, as if to say, 'I would be guilty by association, if I remained part of Israel'. No, they *identified* with their nation. The prayer of an effectual man availeth much! Today the danger is that we would seek to preserve a sense of personal righteousness, and neglect our duty towards the body by saying 'Goodbye' to the body and going our own way.

Conclusion
Fellowship discussion is a difficult exercise. In this chapter I have tried to be careful in my treatment. It is all too easy to throw examples and verses together and draw generalised conclusions. Biblical exposition takes time, and it should be a cooperative effort. We all make mistakes, and it is by discussing these things that we can learn the truth.

Inter-ecclesial relationships, guilt by association and *ecclesial autonomy* have become bones of contention in fellowship discussions. But I think these topics are only the theoretical mask to the underlying problem of *what people feel*. Gut feelings are a significant factor in fellowship matters. People *feel* guilty and *feel* responsible for various things in others, but this varies from person to person. Hence, people collect together in ecclesias with others of a like-mind. All we can do is strive to be *like-minded together* (Rms 15:5, 1 Cor 1:10, 2 Cor 13:11, Phil 1:27, 2:2, 3:16, 1 Pet 3:8) tackling our different feelings. And if we don't associate, how can we begin to be like-minded?

Great divides affect how we can love each other, because such divides mean that we have nothing to do with each other. If some argue that the divides that exist between Christadelphian fellowships are necessary, then one consequence of their view is that *no love* is shared between them and those from other fellowships, and therefore they go square up against the *new commandment*.[1] This is a grave consequence requiring serious reflection, for through this new commandment, all men are meant to *know* the disciples of Christ (Jn 13:34-35). So, are the divides that necessary?

---

[1] This isn't a theoretical point: in lots of local areas, brethren and sisters have nothing to do with other brethren and sisters who live in nearby streets. The situation becomes even more acute in remote African villages, where division has been made to divide people, who really just need to get on with the daily tasks of living the truth and helping each other along the way, taking on the trials that *God* (and not man) places in their way.

CHAPTER FIVE
Ecclesial Discipline

Introduction
In this chapter, I want to examine **discipline in the ecclesia**. Perhaps this is an unpalatable subject to the human mind, but it is a necessary one nonetheless. The substance of my argument will be that there is a real danger today in neglecting discipline, but we need to balance discipline with forbearance and patience. The opposite of discipline is a *laissez faire* attitude that lets things drift along. This may lead to a comfortable life now, but it jeopardises the prospect of eternal life.

The N.T. is our main source of instruction on ecclesial discipline. However, this material gets embroiled in 'fellowship' discussion, so we will need to have an eye on how our subject affects the divisions that exist between Christadelphian ecclesias and fellowships. The chapter is divided into two parts: the first is an expositional journey through the N.T. 'fellowship passages', and the second is a look at how people use these passages in fellowship discussion. The first part concerns facts, while the second part concerns logic and emotion.

In discussing fellowship, *having an eye on how a person is doing his reasoning is very useful*. It's easy to be persuaded by all sorts of factors, and we might end up adopting a view for the wrong reasons. We might be influenced by such things as rhetoric or debating skill, we may be swayed by a powerful personality or family factors, we may be persuaded by an argument while failing to see its weaknesses, *and so on* (cf. Rms 16:18). It's useful then to devote some time to thinking about the logic[1] of people's thinking, and how emotion plays its part in their decisions.

---

[1] God uses logic and He invites us to reason with him, so that our sins might be covered. His word shows the use of logic. So we need to be careful to harness our own fallible use of logic when expounding Biblical teaching.

Describing Christadelphian views on fellowship as either 'conservative' or 'liberal' is fashionable. This can be unhelpful, even if it is a quick and easy way of pigeon-holing people. I find that differences between brethren arise because they emphasize different aspects of the 'doctrine of fellowship', and this is why they get labelled. When all is said and done, brethren who start by emphasizing different things, often end up agreeing on the teaching of the Bible. The differences just need to be thrashed out around a table, a round table.

Discipline in the Ecclesia
Ecclesial discipline is a common Biblical theme, and we neglect it at our peril. The main instrument of Christadelphian discipline has been *withdrawal of fellowship*, but this practice should not blind us to seeing quite a variety of disciplinary actions in the Bible. It is our task to examine this variety.

Discipline requires a sense of responsibility on the part of elders in the ecclesia (1 Tim 3:1-7, Tit 1:5-11), and for their part, the ecclesia needs to be made up of those who recognise that they are part of a group where there are standards to follow (Hebs 13:7,17). Stacked against the exercise of discipline, we have the forces of the world. It's difficult to sum these up, but they represent a *laissez faire* egalitarian view of how groups should be organised.

In our day, the ecclesia ought to be a radical social alternative. It ought to be a separate society, but too often people compartmentalize their lives so that their membership of an ecclesia is just a Sunday affair. If this has happened, discipline will not be welcomed. A sermon once a week, and a charitable donation, is about all that the flesh will bear in such a case.

Our enquiry into this subject comes in two stages: we will first consider those disciplinary actions that *fall short* of withdrawal and separation, i.e. those actions that take place in the ecclesia, and then we will look at the topics of withdrawal and separation. It may be a surprise to think that there are disciplinary actions that fall short of withdrawal, but there are, and if we neglect them in favour of withdrawal, we are failing to make ecclesial discipline match the problem in a person's life.

Actions falling short of Withdrawal[1]

Disciplinary action is of two kinds: **corrective action** and **protective action**. One action seeks to correct the individual; the other seeks to protect the ecclesia. Must there always be withdrawal, or are there disciplinary actions that fall short of withdrawal and separation? Who is to exercise such discipline? The exercise of responsibility is an important element in ecclesial discipline. Who has responsibility? How do they exercise their duties? What controls and safeguards exist to ensure a just application of discipline?[2] These are our questions.

(1) Beseeching/Exhortation

Paul often corrected ecclesias by **beseeching** them in some way. He beseeches the Corinthians "by the name of the Lord Jesus Christ" (1 Cor 1:10). Elsewhere he beseeches his readers by the "mercies of God" (Rms 12:1), "the meekness and gentleness of Christ" (2 Cor 10:1), and "for the Lord Jesus Christ's sake and for the love of the Spirit" (Rms 15:30). These are strong appeals to right behaviour, and their strength flows from the appeal - *for the sake of Christ*. If men don't do something for Christ, what else can an apostle say? - not much really!

> *Beseeching each other is something we can all do, but it is particularly the responsibility of elders.*

Not all Paul's beseechments have a strong appeal, so our beseechments can have varying intensity. The content of the beseechment is not always corrective (Rms 15:30), but often this is the case. Thus we have Paul beseeching the Corinthians to be united (1 Cor 1:10), to follow his example (1 Cor 4:16), and to submit to the household of Stephanas (1 Cor 16:15-16). He beseeches the Romans to mark those that cause divisions and avoid them (Rms 16:17), and he beseeches Euodias and Syntyche to be reconciled (Phil 4:2).

---

[1] Astonishing as it may seem, the idea that the ecclesia is the natural place for discipline, is not usually put forward today - see how the Law handled some species of uncleanness *within* the camp.

[2] Readers will be aware of Robert Roberts 'Ecclesial Guide' which discusses these topics. Its influence can be seen in the way ecclesias of all fellowships run their affairs.

The Greek word for 'beseech' is *parakaleo*, and it is also rendered **'exhort'**. Paul exhorts brethren to walk by God's commandments, he exhorts 'the brethren' to warn the unruly, and some he exhorts to work and not be idle (1 Thess 4:1, 5:14, 2 Thess 3:12). Titus is instructed to exhort with authority, and such exhortation is linked with the corrective action of rebuking (Tit 2:15). Timothy is counselled to exhort with teaching and longsuffering (2 Tim 4:2). We see then a corrective aspect to exhortation[1] as well as beseeching.

> *Beseeching\exhortation is a fundamental aspect of the work of building up the body of Christ, and is principally aimed at the correction of doctrine and practice. Paul and his fellow-workers practice it, and it became a principal function of elders. It took two forms - a simple beseechment and a beseechment by some authority.*[2]

In these examples of correction, ecclesias, individuals, or specific groups are addressed. This observation prompts the question as to whether ecclesial discipline could be directed to *any kind of audience* as the need arose. Could any action be applied to any person or any group? In fellowship discussions, this question becomes acute when some argue that *withdrawal* can be applied to *global* groups. So, **what is the principle of application** involved in the administration of corrective (and protective) actions? In answering this query, we will find that certain actions are applied to individuals, while others are administered to whole ecclesias and groups within ecclesias. However, we will find little evidence for *global* block withdrawal.

(2) Warning
There are several other forms of corrective activity. **Warning** (Gk: *noutheteo, nouthesia*) is one such form of correction. Paul employs strong language in warning the Corinthian believers not to be "puffed up for one against another", and the warning was designed to bring

---

[1] In those cases where exhortation and beseeching is not corrective, their purpose seems to be purely instructional.
[2] The distinction not only appears to mark the gravity of the situation being addressed, but also the description of the authority seems to be so constructed as to reflect the situation being addressed.

about a change among them (1 Cor 4:14, see v6ff).[1] Other examples of warning include:

- Paul warning the unruly at Thessalonica (1 Thess 3)

- Paul's ministry at Ephesus, where warning was an important and regular part of his activity (Acts 20:31)

In thinking of what warning means today, considering the analogy of fathers warning children is helpful (Eph 6:4, cf. 1 Cor 10:11).[2]

> *Notice one feature of this action of warning: in the examples given we see that it is directed both towards individuals and to a whole ecclesia. We can't restrict this instrument of discipline to individuals or groups, and indeed a great deal of warning is made in ecclesial magazines and from platforms today.*

Paul's practice was to send his representatives to ecclesias as the need arose.[3] Thus Titus was to correct believers at Corinth (2 Cor 7, nb. v14), and rebuke and reject heretics and subverters on the island of Crete. Timothy was to reprove and rebuke at Ephesus (1 Tim 4:2-5), and to correct at Corinth (1 Cor 4:17, 16:10). In the Pastoral Epistles we have Paul's explicit guidance to these two roving representatives. We don't have 'apostolic authority' today, but the practice of sending envoys to ecclesias with trouble is often seen in the missionary field, and such people are often called upon to get involved in settling local disputes.

---

[1] Supplementing this (beseeching and) warning, he sends an envoy to teach them, which is an important part of his corrective dealings, and something for us to consider.

[2] Closely related to this action of warning there is the corrective action of **chastening**, or disciplinary instruction. We shall look at this action shortly.

[3] Notice a need arises in an area before Paul sends envoys to exercise correction. This is a different wisdom to one which exports doctrinal trouble to places where brethren and sisters have not thought of the issue.

(3) Charging and Commanding
Those who have rulership in an ecclesia can counter false teaching in several ways. They are *not* restricted to just the one course of action - withdrawal.

Timothy was commanded to **charge** some not to teach different and unprofitable doctrine (A.V. "other" doctrine, Gk: *heteros*). Evidently, at Ephesus some were interested in fables, genealogies, and debates, wanting to be teachers of the law, and such Timothy was to *charge* not to teach (1 Tim 1:3-4). This charge is given *first mention* in his letter, and from this we may infer that it was very important, so much so, it was committed to Timothy according to prophecies (1 Tim 1:18).

What was a charge? It would seem that a charge was some sort of requirement laid upon a person in some way before the Lord (2 Tim 2:14, cf. 1 Tim 5:21). In 1 Tim 5, the financial support of widows was to be given in "charge", which suggests that such a requirement had a *binding nature*. The uses of the Greek word translated "charge" in Acts 5:28 (cf. v40) and Acts 16:24 reinforce this view. In those instances, the contexts relate to the administration of the law of the land. In all of these cases, the purpose of these charges, (we might say orders), is to correct behaviour.

A charge is given in response to a situation that needs correction. *Charging* seems a neglected instrument of ecclesial discipline today. In our egalitarian age, ecclesial elders may be reluctant to tell someone to stop teaching a certain doctrine, but it has been done in the past. If someone heeds the charge, then this shows a submissive spirit. A person may not immediately give up their view, but their submission to a charge will allow discussion of their doctrine to continue quietly. Their submission shows *teachableness*.

The Greek for "charge" (*parangelia* and *parangello*) can carry the weaker sense of **commanding**, which is also associated with correction in the epistles. In 1 Cor 11:17, we have a clear example of a corrective response to abuses surrounding the Lords Supper. Paul says, "Now in this that I *command* you, I praise you not, you come together not for the better but for the worse." Another example is found in 2 Thess 3 (vs 6, 12), where Paul deals with disorderly brethren with a commandment 'in the name of the Lord Jesus Christ'.

Clearly, then, commanding[1] was a form of ecclesial correction in certain contexts. How do charges differ from commands? How are they applied? Here we may observe that whereas our examples of charges relate to *individuals*, commands relate *also* to larger numbers - whole ecclesias. Apart from this difference, charges seem to be more forceful.

(4) Reproof and Rebuke
Two other kinds of ecclesial discipline are **reproofs** and **rebukes**. Timothy was to reprove and rebuke, with all longsuffering and doctrine, those who turned away from the truth unto fables and other teachers. Reproof and rebuke were part of Timothy's general armoury against declension from the Gospel. What was a reproof or a rebuke?

Almost all examples of **rebukes** (Gk: *epitimao*, epitimia) occur in the Gospels, and in three kinds of context.

a) The most interesting context, from our point of view, is that where a person rebukes another *for something said*. Thus we see Christ rebuking the crowds and his disciples for attempting to make him more famous. Peter rebuked Christ for talking of his forthcoming sacrifice, and Jesus rebuked Peter for so doing. On the way to Jericho, the multitude is recorded as rebuking two blind men for crying out for Jesus to heal them. Christ rebuked James and John for suggesting that they command fire to come down from heaven and consume the Samaritans. The Pharisees suggested once that the praise of Jesus' disciples should be rebuked, and the thief on the cross rebuked his friend.[2]

b) The other major use of 'rebuke' is the rebuking of devils and unclean spirits. Significantly, this rebuking of devils and spirits takes

---

[1] Other instances of commands lay down rules of behaviour (e.g. 1 Cor 7). Yet a further example of a corrective command is Eph 5:28, "Let him that stole, steal no more, rather let him labour..." This utterance of Paul's is directed towards a specific kind of situation that would require correction. More examples could be given.
[2] See Matt 12:16, cf. Mk 3:12; Matt 16:20, cf. Lk 9:22; Matt 16:22, 20:31, cf. Mk 10:48; Mk 8:33; Lk 9:59, 18:39, 19:39, 23:30.

place in a context of the *noise and clamour* created by such persons (Lk 4:35, 39, 41).

c) The third and only other kind of rebuke is of the raging winds and sea.

It is no surprise then to find the corrective action of rebuke applied to those *who would speak* vain things.

On one occasion, Paul was much grieved in having to write to the Corinthians about a certain man, who had done something requiring a 'rebuke'. (The A.V. translates the Greek word with "punishment"). We do not know the problem underlying this heaviness of heart expressed by Paul, but we can gather that it was *verbal behaviour* of some sort. However, we are told that the censure was sufficient unto its purpose, and that now love should be shown towards the man (2 Cor 2:6-7). Here Paul shows two important aspects of ecclesial discipline:

- the idea of an action being *sufficient*

- the idea of *follow-up care* for the offender

Notice here that these rebukes are applied *individually*, in contrast to the actions of exhortation, commanding and warning which are general.

What is reproof (Gk: *elegcho*)?[1] **Reproof** is an important element of ecclesial correction, and exercised by elders (Tit 1:7-9). It was applicable to all, even elders that sinned, and it was to induce *fear* (1 Tim 5:20). This indicates the force of a reproof, (as well as indicating that elders were amenable to ecclesial discipline). Titus was to reprove those who contradicted, with sound doctrine, and in a manner that was sharp and authoritative (Tit 1:11, 13, 2:15). The aim was to stop

---

[1] The Greek word is translated "reproof" in 2 Tim 4:2, but it is generally rendered in the A.V. by "rebuke", which blurs the distinction between reproof and rebuke. We will, however, use the word "reproof" to translate the Greek *elegcho*.

the offence in question, a similar purpose to the charge mentioned in 1 Tim 1:3.

We see then some qualities of reproof: **it was authoritative and, on occasion, sharp.**

A reproof shows something for what it is: a reproof is therefore different from a rebuke. Here are some examples of how the word is used:

- The deeds of those in darkness are *shown up* by the light (Jn 3:20, Eph 5:11, 13).

- The erring brother is to be *shown* his fault, and Herod was *shown* up for his sins by John (Matt 18:16, Lk 3:19).

- The law *shows* forth those who transgress (Jms 2:19).

Accordingly, those who contradicted apostolic teaching would be shown for what they were by sound doctrine.[1] In our egalitarian age, perhaps we are reluctant to reprove or rebuke brethren and sisters. Somehow, we have to balance such actions with love and forbearance.

(5) Instruction
Instruction (Gk: *paideuo*) is another corrective action. For example, those who opposed themselves were to be instructed in the hope that they would repent and acknowledge the truth (2 Tim 2:25). Jesus instructed (A.V. "taught") men to forsake ungodliness, worldly lusts, and live sober righteous lives (Tit 2:12).

What does *paideuo* mean? The word is related to a Greek word for a child, and it conjures up an image of the disciplinary instruction[2]

---

[1] Examples of reproof and rebuke abound in the epistles, even though the words we have been looking at are infrequent. See for instance, 1 Cor 3:1 and 6:5.
[2] By contrast, the Greek for "teaching" (*didasko*) does not occur in close association with corrective needs, but rather with the need to impart knowledge.

administered to children. Thus we read that if believers endure *chastening*, it is as *sons* that God regards them (Hebs 12:6-8). Accordingly, Jesus rebuked and chastened Laodicea, and declared that it was *as many as he loved* that he chastened (Rev 3:19, cf. 1 Cor 11:32). Where we read that Paul handed over Hymenaeus and Alexander to Satan that they may "learn" not to blaspheme (1 Tim 1:20), we may infer that a disciplinary kind of instruction is intended.

Separation, Withdrawal and False Doctrine

We now turn to consider separation and withdrawal in relation to false doctrine. Most fellowship discussion in this area revolves around a group of N.T. 'withdrawal' passages. As we look at these, we need to have a few questions in mind:

- are the 'withdrawal' passages applied to individuals, groups within ecclesias, or (global) blocks of ecclesias?

- is the responsibility to 'withdraw' for the whole ecclesia, or all ecclesias in the global church, or for individuals?

- do the 'withdrawal' passages all amount to the same kind of action, or are there different kinds of 'withdrawal'?

- how are the 'withdrawal' passages to be applied today?

The questions are ones we cannot ignore. Christadelphians are divided into various 'fellowships', and one justification made for this state of affairs goes (roughly) like this:

> *'there are (many) errors in the 'other' fellowships, and you must keep separate from them as the N.T. passages on 'withdrawal' show, otherwise the errors will grow and take over people's thinking'*

This argument is (usually) made by smaller fellowships against their bigger neighbours. The argument is made at the time of a division, and it is perpetuated for as long as the emerging fellowship continues to exist. Before a division there will have been one fellowship, afterwards there are at least two fellowships. One of the fellowships will retain the identity of the old unified fellowship, while the other will assume another identity. Usually, this identity is supplied by the title of a new or current fellowship magazine.[1] The new fellowship will make the argument that the old fellowship has those holding or teaching error 'in' it, and it is necessary to separate, not only from these false teachers, but also those in that fellowship who refuse to make an appropriate stand against the errors.[2] This *fear* is one that must be respected, but is global block withdrawal *the only solution* to the problem of false teaching? Or again, is global block withdrawal possible when the number of ecclesias is so large, or where there is no central authority?

(1) Rejection, Withdrawal, Stopping and Avoidance
The main trouble affecting the N.T. ecclesias was the Jewish counter-reformation, against which the elders and apostles employed a variety of measures. In the Pastoral Epistles, Paul advises Timothy and Titus on how to handle the Jewish sectarians in Asia Minor and Crete, and the actions he counsels are set out in Figure 1. These actions are clearly addressed to the same kind of situation, but it is not one that is familiar to us today, so we have to *apply* the principles implicit in Paul's counsel. We have already examined the actions of charging, reproving and rebuking; now we want to think of *avoidance, rejection* and *withdrawal.*

Sectarianism was at the root of Paul's concern, for this was the way that the Jews were undermining the church.[3] There were two elements to this challenge: firstly, there were the false teachers, and secondly, there were those who followed them. The situations were serious, for the adjectives Paul uses to describe them are severe (e.g. 1 Tim 4:2,

---

[1] Examples of this include, the *Advocate* fellowship, the *Fraternal Visitor* fellowship, the *Berean* fellowship, the *Dawn* fellowship, the *Remnant*, the *Watchman* fellowship, and others.
[2] Take four fellowships, A, B, C, D, each of which divides from the fellowship preceding it in the sequence, i.e. fellowship B divides from A, fellowship C divides from B, and fellowship D divides from C. In fellowship discussion, each fellowship will use this argument against the fellowship from which it has divided, i.e. D uses it against C, C uses it against B and B uses it against A.
[3] See Acts 20:30, Gal 3:1ff, Col 2:19-22, 1 Tim 1:3,6, 4:1-3, 2 Tim 4:3-4, Tit 1:10-11, 3:12).

6:4-5, Tit 1:11, 15-16). Paul's instructions are simple: those who *taught* Jewish doctrine were to be charged not to teach, or their mouths were to be stopped (1 Tim 1:3, Tit 1:11). The objectives were to make them sound in the faith through sound doctrine (Tit 1:9, 13), and to protect the ecclesia (Tit 1:11). His personal counsel to Titus and Timothy was to avoid such doctrine and to withdraw[1] themselves from such teachers (1 Tim 4:7, 6:3-5, 2 Tim 2:23, Tit 3:9). Those who followed these teachers were to be admonished (twice, if need be - maybe the sectarian is willing to be quiet and be taught, and if so he is given a chance to stop promoting the sect), and then (if need be) 'rejected' (Tit 3:10) - they were heretics.[23]

avoid, reject and withdraw from those who	charge not to teach those who	stop those who teach
ask foolish questions, dispute genealogies, strive about the law, and are vain talkers	minister questions, endless genealogies, desiring to be teachers of the law, fond of vain jangling and fables	Commandments of men, and are vain, and fond of Jewish fables
Titus 3:9-10, 1 Tim 6:3-5	1 Tim 1:3ff	Titus 1:9ff

Figure 1: Jewish Counter-Reformation

---

[1] What does the term "withdrawal" (Gk: *aphistemi*) mean? It carries the sense of "depart" or "leave" as those words are used in describing a departure of someone or the leaving of something alone (Acts 12:10, 15:38, 22:25, cf. 1 Tim 4:1, 2 Tim 2:19, Hebs 3:12).
[2] Are these adjectives applicable to Christadelphians in other fellowships? If they are not applicable, can we use these 'withdrawal' texts to justify division?
[3] A heretic is one who promotes or is part of a sect - a sectarian. The word 'sect' (Gk: *hairesis*) is found in such phrases as "the *sect* of the Sadducees" (Acts 5:17, 15:5, 26:5), which was a sect of the religion of Judaism. For Jews, Christianity was a *sect* (Acts 24:5), and Paul seems to accept this appellation (Acts 24:15). In 1 Cor 11:19-20, Paul notes that there were *sects* at Corinth (A.V. "heresies"), and in Gal 5:20, Paul lists *sects* as a work of the flesh (cf. 1 Cor 3:3).

Paul gives us an example of what it is to depart (same Greek word as 'withdrawal') from non-Christians, who speak evil of the way (cf. 1 Tim 6:4, and the phrase "evil surmising"), in his departure from the Ephesian synagogue (Acts 19:8). Having associated with the synagogue for three months, the Jews became hardened, and spoke evil of Christianity. Thus Paul departed from them, *and separated* the disciples who were also in association with the synagogue.[1] In 1 Tim 6, Paul may have had this case in mind when advising Timothy.[2]

A comparable example of a protective action counselled by Paul is contained in Rms 16:17-18. Those who cause seditions (Gk: *dichostasia*, cf. Gal 5:20) and offences (Gk: *skandalon*) are to be *avoided*. They carry out the works of the flesh, and display their unworthiness for God's kingdom. An example of such was the Balaamites who were casting a stumbling block before the ecclesia at Pergamos in the form of a doctrine of promiscuity. The phrase, "serve their own belly", in Rms 16:18 carries the sense of immorality, as it does in 1 Cor 6:13. Such people were to be avoided (Gk: *ekklino* cf. 1 Pet 3:11, 2 Jn 10, 11), being the enemies of the cross of Christ.

These actions, *rejection, withdrawal, stopping, and avoidance*, concern *three types of person*, and we shouldn't treat these kinds of individual in the same way. We need to be sensitive with those who are led astray, while being firm with those who would seek to change the basis of faith:

---

[1] Modern Christadelphians might think that they are one sect in a wider Christendom, but it would appear that we ought to think of ourselves as a sect of Judaism.

[2] An interesting observation regarding the incidents of Acts 19 is relevant. Paul is described as departing, whereas the disciples are described as being separated by Paul. In 1 Tim 6 there is no corresponding separation, but it is likely that there would have been such a separation by Timothy in respect of the Ephesian ecclesia. In both examples, the protective duties of elders are clearly manifest.

- false teachers are to be charged and stopped, with the hope that they may learn sound doctrine, or the teacher is to be removed (kept away from) from the ecclesia

- church leaders are to keep themselves away from false teachers,[1] and the ecclesia is to be separated from the source of the false teaching if necessary

- a sectarian is to be given a second chance and then refused[234]

There is no reason not to apply this counsel today, when the circumstances dictate, but when have modern circumstances required such action? The way to answer this question is to see if the situation Paul describes matches modern situations in some way. Paul faced Jewish problems, but we can't dismiss the example just because Christadelphians haven't had (or got) Jewish problems in their midst. Here is a list of the attributes of those leading the Jewish attack and their followers:

contradiction of sound doctrine	contention and strife
subversion of house churches	foolish questions
motivation by love of money	lack of understanding
defilement	lies and hypocrisy
abominableness	a seared conscience
disobedience	reprobate
destitute of truth	perverse
corrupt	objectors to Christ

---

[1] We might add that in addition to leaders avoiding false teachers, the ecclesia also should remove them. Such 'sect-formers' need to be *removed* from the body (i.e. *moved away from the body* Rms 16:17).

[2] Those who subvert houses are a different to those who are subverted. Paul is concerned with the subverters in Titus 1 and with the subverted in Titus 3 (v11).

[3] The Greek word for 'reject' (Gk: *paraiteomai*) is directed towards *what people are saying* and it is a refusal of *them* in some way (Lk 14:18,19, Acts 25:11, 1 Tim 4:7, 5:11, 2 Tim 2:23, Hebs 12:19, 25).

[4] This mention of two admonitions may indicate that they are *Christian* heretics, but we cannot be certain.

This kind of scenario is one where a competing and established religion clashes with true Christianity, but sustaining the view that Christadelphian fellowships are like this would be difficult. It would be hard to justify the view that the sort of descriptions used by Paul of the Jewish counter-reformation are equally applicable to other Christadelphian fellowships.[1]

The onslaught of the Jewish attack may be absent today, but we must still ask what lessons there are for us to learn, and doctrine is the common ingredient that we have to consider. There are problems faced by Christadelphian fellowships today which give cause for concern. The churches of Christendom present the most basic challenge, and this is one which is ecumenical and evangelical in character (see Chapter Three). We can expect this problem to emerge among the ecclesias, and we can expect ecclesias to be subverted in the process. Such a situation as this would be one partly comparable to the situation faced by the apostles.

Today the ecclesial leaders should be vigilant towards false doctrines and false teachers. In our easy-going age, this is difficult, but a clear perception of the faith once delivered to the saints is essential. Like the apostles, they are faced with an ecclesial world in which these problems manifest themselves in different places at different times. To an outsider the church will appear mixed, but this is inevitable, as Paul says, schisms must occur amongst us, so that those who are approved will be made manifest (1 Cor 11:19).[2] The N.T. information that we have concerns ecclesias and the problems that assailed them.

---

[1] Christadelphian troubles have revolved around such things as divorce and re-marriage, the doctrine of the atonement, non-combatant military service - these are different kinds of trouble to those problems of the first century.

[2] The reason why such false teachers emerge is supplied in the Law: the Lord aims to prove us, to see whether we love him, i.e. believe him (Deut 13:3). If we are to expect such tests, we can certainly learn from the apostles on how they handled their tests, even if ours are different. Peter says that false teachers would arise *within* the church and form sects (2 Pet 2:1, cf. Acts 20:30, 2 Tim 4:3-4).

Christadelphian divisions have come about by the procedure of ecclesias 'banding together' into a new group, which then breaks away. Such a procedure has no N.T. precedent, because the examples we have are all local and ecclesial in their focus. How do you apply protective actions such as withdrawal, rejection, avoidance and stopping? Some justify block withdrawal by extending the N.T. examples: they say that if a false teacher or a group in one locality is withdrawn from, as the Pastoral Epistles show, then withdrawal can be spread to other areas, and brethren and sisters all over the world can be invited to make a decision on any local dispute.[1] The spirit behind block withdrawal is to re-establish a sound (pure) global church, through a clean break, which then stands as a competing example to the 'failing' fellowship.[2]

Paul placed the onus upon the local elders. In the case of Rms 16, Paul is addressing the "brethren" at Rome. He instructs that they were to mark those that cause divisions and 'avoid' them. We may infer that this action was for those in positions of responsibility, who had the protective care of the flock (Acts 20:31, 1 Thess 5:12ff, 2 Thess 3:6ff). It was the same for Timothy, who was charged with the care of the Ephesian ecclesia, when he was instructed to 'withdraw' from teachers of other doctrine. However, Titus was in Crete, and he was given responsibility over the *whole island*, i.e. all the city ecclesias of the island (Tit 1:5). When Paul counsels him to 'stop' the mouths of the gainsayers, and 'reject' sectarians, we can be certain that he carried this out throughout the island.

It is, then, no good arguing that dealing with false doctrine is *solely* an ecclesial responsibility, as if to say, an ecclesia is a self-contained watertight unit. The example of the apostles and their helpers shows that the body of Christ needs inter-ecclesial leadership, and such leaders have a responsibility to protect the body in the wider sense. Nevertheless, what we can say is that such figures dealt with problems as they arose at the *local level*. We don't have any evidence that they

---

[1] Some Christadelphian disputes (and divisions) have been nothing like the counter-reformation that the apostles combated.
[2] The Angel of the Lord proposed to make a clean break and establish a sound congregation through Moses, but Moses refused.

went *any further* and instituted global division, by getting all worldwide ecclesias to divide up on a given question.

(2) To have or not to have
Withdrawal has been the main instrument of ecclesial discipline, but there are other actions we must consider. The letters to the Revelation ecclesias are always considered in this context.[1] They talk about our attitudes to false doctrine, and they talk about 'having and not having' false teachers and sects within our midst. From the letters we learn,

- we are to *hate* certain practices, e.g. Nicolaitan kinds of behaviour (Ephesus)

- we must not *have* among us those who hold certain doctrines, e.g. Balaamites or Nicolaitans doctrine (Pergamos)

- we must not *tolerate* false 'prophets' like Jezebel (Thyatira)

The ecclesias of Christ, today, do not have these particular doctrines or practices, but we need to take on board the right attitudes towards such grave false doctrines. Frankly put, we need to be *intolerant* of false teachers, and not *have* amongst us those who are allied to party positions on false doctrine.[2]

The seven ecclesias were in Christ's hand, even though some were in a spiritually poor state. This is not to say that they would always remain in his hand *no matter what happened*. He warns the Laodicean

---

[1] In passing, observe that sending a letter can be corrective and protective, just as much as personal contact. The inter-ecclesial action of Acts 15 involved sending a letter, but note that emissaries were commissioned to "take" the letter (thereby upholding the principle of personal relevance). Likewise, Paul sent several letters with emissaries, and saw the value of this approach (2 Cor 7:8, 10:9-10).

[2] I am not saying that fellowships or ecclesias will not have those who teach false doctrine from time to time. We know the body of Christ will be mixed - the point is that we ought to be at war with the flesh. It is a mistake to think that we can eliminate the enmity between the spirit and the flesh in ecclesial life by creating pure fellowships.

ecclesia that he would 'spew' them out of his mouth (Rev 3:16), and he warns the Ephesian ecclesia that their candlestick would be removed unless they repented (Rev 2:5). Neither should we say that just because the bad ecclesias were in Christ's hand at that time, they were fit for fellowship in the church. The warnings might have been to each individual ecclesia, but they were recorded for all ecclesias (Rev 2:11,29, 3:6,13,22). So each ecclesia in Asia was to know the state of the other ecclesias and be suitably warned.[1]

Nevertheless, what we do learn from these letters is that the body of Christ will have ecclesias in its midst in differing states of health. Further, we learn that to be a member of an ecclesia that has such problems is possible. We would not be guilty by that formal association. For example, Sardis had some worthy saints who had not defiled their garments (Rev 3:4).[2] In Thyatira, some had not yielded to the doctrines of Jezebel, (like the 7000 in the days of Elijah), and they were counselled to hold fast till Christ came to them (Rev 2:25). The ecclesias are addressed as collective entities, but a difference was made between the faithful and unfaithful in the ecclesias.

If we take the seven ecclesias and think of them as Christadelphian ecclesias, we might like to think we are Philadelphia or Smyrna. On the other hand, it is possible that the other ecclesias are represented amongst us as well.[3] Pergamos and Thyatira had some good and some bad points. Laodicea was in a dreadful state, and Ephesus was not much better. How do we think of the various Christadelphian fellowships? Are all the good ecclesias in one fellowship, and all the bad ecclesias in another fellowship? Or is it, rather, that there are sound ecclesias with faithful brethren and sisters in all fellowships? If this is

---

[1] This happens today when an ecclesia is subverted by a false doctrine or teaching, because it's not long before other sound ecclesias become aware of this and take appropriate action.

[2] These saints are addressed as **in** Sardis, so they must be recognised as part of the ecclesia at least in a formal sense, although it is fair to assume that they would have had to dis-associate from rest of the ecclesia in practical ways.

[3] One survey (1992) estimates there are 864 ecclesias and representatives of the main fellowship worldwide.

the case, where is the justification in the Revelation letters for the present divided state of Christadelphians?

(3) Failure to withdraw

Ecclesias will fail to withdraw, and they will make mistakes in their judgements. Ecclesias will go after false teachers and be subverted. What should be the response of faithful ecclesias? We have no specific N.T. precedents of how ecclesias should react to the failure of other ecclesias to withdraw from false teachers. But the lesson of the 'withdrawal' passages must surely be that ecclesial leaders would need to protect their own ecclesia from an unfaithful ecclesia.[1] This response could be taken in a variety of ways:

- ecclesias might be remote from the unfaithful ecclesia, and therefore merely note the relevant facts of the case

- ecclesias might cease to exchange visiting brethren[2] with the unfaithful ecclesia, they may warn their members of the problems in the unfaithful ecclesia

- ecclesias might reinforce their basis of assembly, and inform other ecclesias that they oppose the unfaithful ecclesia

- ecclesias might issue a formal notice of withdrawal to the unfaithful ecclesia

The last action is thought by some ecclesias to be the *only* proper response to the circumstance of there being unfaithful ecclesias in the body. This view has led to block divisions, because those sound ecclesias, who fail to issue formal notices of withdrawal to unfaithful ecclesias, have themselves become the subject of notices of withdrawal.

Should withdrawal become an inter-ecclesial instrument of discipline? We have no specific N.T. examples of such a disciplinary measure.

---

[1] Ecclesias will fail to withdraw, but what about sound ecclesias who fail to withdraw from ecclesias who fail to withdraw?
[2] We discussed 2 John vv. 10-11 in Chapter Four.

Perhaps all we can say is that ecclesias ought to recognise unfaithful ecclesias and take some measures to protect their flock, but the wisdom of local elders will vary on what action is appropriate to their own circumstances, which may amount to withdrawal in some cases.

Sinful Behaviour and Withdrawal
We have been considering withdrawal in connection with false teaching, and we now turn to think of withdrawal and immoral behaviour.

(1) Shunning a person
Paul commands the Thessalonians brethren (elders, cf. 1 Thess 5) to withdraw themselves from every brother that walketh disorderly and not after his tradition (2 Thess 3:6, cf. 2 Thess 2:15). In these verses, the Thessalonians are reminded that they were to work, and not be dependent on others, but to support themselves (cf. 1 Thess 1:5-6, nb. Paul's reference to his manner of life). In this context, then, "disorderly" means a life not *ordered* by work. Elsewhere, Paul had exhorted believers to follow his example in life, namely, to work with their own hands (1 Cor 4:16, see v 12).

What does it mean to 'withdraw' (Gk: *stellomai*)[1] from a disorderly brother? The word *stellomai* has the sense of avoiding a consequence (cf. 2 Cor 8:20). In 2 Thess 3, the A.V. translation would appear reasonable, as withdrawing oneself from a person is an act of avoidance or shunning. Paul is therefore commanding the brethren to keep away from idle busybodies. We cannot tell from this instruction, however, whether Paul is enjoining some *formal* ecclesial action, or whether he is commanding the brethren to keep away from busybodies on an individual (or some other) basis. Later in Paul's letter (3:14), we are given another expression for this action of 'withdrawal' - "have no company" (Gk: *sunanamignumi*, cf. 1 Cor 5:9).[2] A paraphrase of Paul's counsel would go something like this:

---

[1] This word is clearly different from that used in 1 Tim 6:5. Apart from this, the issue being dealt with here, is completely different to that addressed by 1 Tim 6. There is therefore no reason to connect the two passages as examples of the very same action.

[2] This action is not an action to take if people fail to withdraw, but a re-statement of the need to 'withdraw' from the idle busybodies.

> *There are some whose walk among you is disorderly. These we command and exhort that with quietness (instead of being busybodies (see 1 Thess 4:11)) they work (instead of not working) and eat their own bread, and if any man obey not our word (in this matter) by this letter, note that man, and have no company with him, so that he might be ashamed.*

Some propose that a formal ecclesial action is enjoined here, others suggest individual action is being counselled. It can't be a purely individual matter, because Paul's command is to *everyone* in the ecclesia,[1] but this fact doesn't mean it is a formal ecclesial action. However, the action *was to have limited effect*, because the brother was still to be admonished "as a brother" (v15). Within the social structure of the church, such a limitation would mean that the elders, who had the characteristic duty of admonishment, were to keep regular contact and extend pastoral care to the brother. It seems possible that they would share the emblems with him, outside the framework of the ecclesia coming together to break bread (1 Jn 2:9-10, 3:23, Jn 13:31-35). Insofar as there is some kind of pastoral care directed towards the brother(s) involved, it would follow that they were still to be regarded as *part* (i.e. members) of the local ecclesia.[2]

(2) Having no company and putting away
There was an incestuous fornicator in the Corinthian ecclesia and the ecclesia hadn't done anything about this fact. This was a scandal and accordingly, Paul gives detailed and unusual instructions on a corrective procedure:

> *Such a person was to be delivered unto Satan for the destruction of the flesh, so that the spirit might be saved in the day of the Lord (1 Cor 5:5).*

---

[1] The avoidance of someone varies according to the social structure of which those involved are a part. In a small social structure, such as that of a club or society, it may truly be said that 'x' is avoiding 'y', even though they are present in the society or club.
[2] It has to be said that the good of the individual can be lost in a desire to have a pure church.

This statement is perhaps difficult to understand, and there are several suggested interpretations. One proposal is that incest was a capital crime, and the ecclesia is being instructed to hand over the person to Satan (the state authorities) for punishment. Another view suggests that the destruction of the flesh refers to a physical punishment inflicted at some gathering of the ecclesia, by the power of the Lord Jesus Christ (cf. 1 Tim 1:19-20). We do not have this power today, so any lessons for us must lie in another direction.

Paul had already written previously on the matter: the Corinthians had failed to dissociate from this fornicator (1 Cor 5:9-11).[1] So now Paul forcefully instructed them to put away, (not have company with, Gk: *sunanamignumi*, cf. 2 Thess 3:14), the wicked person, and *in addition* deliver the person to Satan (1 Cor 5:4-5, 11, 13). Clearly, this action has social implications, and the social context that Paul uses for his illustration is 'the feast'.[2] The action was intended to correct the offender, and protect the standards of the ecclesia. The figure of leavening the whole lump graphically pictures the influences that bad morals have in social groups. Consequently, if that leaven[3] is taken out, the influence is checked.

Here, unlike our previous examples, we have a new dimension to consider. Not only do we see Paul stating what must be done about a *particular person*, but we also see him advising on *why* the person needs to be removed. In discussing the 'why', Paul's thinking is more abstract, and he employs a figure of speech. We learn from this example that we too must think of the reasons for 'withdrawal', and when we begin to think of *reasons* (rather than people), our thinking becomes more abstract.

---

[1] Failure to withdraw is a common question in fellowship discussion. How do we react to this failure? Paul's reaction was to *re-iterate* the need for withdrawal.

[2] This feast might be a Jewish feast (vv. 7-8), or more probably the breaking of bread, which was part of a fraternal meal (1 Cor 11), or the fraternal meals that the ecclesia might enjoy.

[3] Elsewhere, this figure is used of a false doctrine of salvation which was affecting the Galatian ecclesias (Gal 1:6-8, 3:1-2, 5:1-12, 6:12, cf. Acts 15:1ff).

> *The reasons for 'withdrawal' are simple: we need to avoid the influence of immoral behaviour and false doctrine. (Notice how 1 Cor 5:13 quotes Deut 13:5).*

Paul involved the *whole ecclesia* (cf. 1 Tim 5:20) in this action of 'withdrawal', because they were all culpable in some way. They were to carry out the action 'when they came together' (probably before a memorial meeting), and with the power of the Lord, they were to 'deliver the person to Satan'. In today's terms, the action was a *formal ecclesial action*, and this distinguishes the case from that in 2 Thess 3. What do we learn from 1 Cor 5? We learn that the ecclesia must have no company with those who live in an immoral state. The example is incest, but equally grave examples would include adultery, fornication, and general sexual immorality. We learn that the 'withdrawal' is an *ecclesial* action and not just an action for individuals. We also learn that an ecclesia can be guilty if it does not carry out 'withdrawal'.

In discussing this *ecclesial* dimension, we must not forget that there is also much emphasis in the epistles on the theme of *personal protection* - looking after your own welfare. Fornication is to be avoided (1 Cor 7:1, 1 Thess 4:3ff), abstention from the appearance of evil is necessary (1 Thess 5:22), participation in the sins of others forbidden, and so on (1 Tim 5:22). These personal directives are protective insofar as they counsel people to erect spiritual barriers against sin.

We have now examined actions described as *refusing* (Tit 3:10), *leaving alone* (1 Tim 6), *avoidance* (Rms 16), *withdrawal* (2 Thess 3) and *not keeping company with a believer* (1 Cor 5). These actions relate to different kinds of case. One relates to factious sectarians, another relates to those opposing the moral teaching of Christ, whilst the last relates to waywardness in the life of a believer. It would seem that the differences in each situation meant that a different response was required. They are all examples relating to the discipline of church members.

Separation
The action of *separation* is another 'fellowship' action, and it is detailed in terms of a contrast between light and darkness - between those who are "of the temple of God" and those who are outside (2 Cor 6:14-17). It is not an action directed towards individuals *in* the church, but an action that brings about a *state of separation* from false religion.

To be in fellowship with God it is necessary to walk in the light, and be separate from darkness.

What does this mean? The word 'darkness' occurs in two kinds of context:

- One context is that of the Jewish religious order and society (Matt 4:16, Lk 1:79, 22:53, Jn 1:5, 2 Cor 4:6, Col 1:13, 1 Jn 2:8).

- The other context is that of the Gentile world and its behaviour (Acts 26:18, Rms 2:19, 13:12, 1 Cor 4:5, 2 Cor 6:14, Eph 5:11).

To walk in darkness is therefore to walk in unbelief and immorality be this Jewish or Gentile (Acts 26:23). With such we are to have no fellowship and be separate (2 Cor 6:14, Eph 5:11).

As Gentiles living in these last days, we might readily agree to the principle of separation from the world, but how do we apply the 1c. principle of separation from the Jewish religious order?

The apostle John thinks of darkness (Gk: *skotia*) as the Jewish world and its religious order and society. Paul speaks more generally of the Gentile order of things (Acts 13:47). John connects *walking in the light* with the **Gospel**:

> "If that which ye have heard from the beginning shall remain in you, ye shall continue in the Father and the Son" (1 Jn 2:24).

The message was that "God is light and in him is no darkness at all" (1 Jn 1:1,5), It concerned the "Word of Life", which was manifest in Christ (1 Jn 1:1,4). Jesus was the Light and glory of God (Jn 1:1-18), and acceptance of this was the basis of apostolic fellowship (1 Jn 1:3). To let this Gospel message abide in us is to walk in the light.

It would seem then that the counsel to walk in the light and to have no fellowship with this kind of darkness has an application today with regard to *other 'Christian'* denominations. If other churches do not preach the apostolic gospel, and worship God in a spirit of falsehood and, moreover, condemn the body of Christ's brethren in their preaching, then it would seem that they are modern-day counterparts to the Jews' stance towards the fellowship of the apostles.

Summary
Let us summarise the results of our study so far.

- The application of ecclesial discipline was for local elders. We may call this the **principle of ecclesial autonomy**.

- The sphere in which corrective and protective action is applied is the ecclesia. We call this the **principle of ecclesial jurisdiction**.

- Discipline is applied to *only* those who are responsible and guilty.[1] We may call this the **principle of relevance**.

- There are various disciplinary actions from which we can choose. Some are applied to *individuals*[2] and some are applicable to *groups*.[3] We may call this the **principle of fitness** - discipline is made appropriate and fitting to the problem in hand.

How do we apply discipline today? Our Bible teaching has come in the form of examples rather than general laws. So we have to compare our problem situations today with the examples of the first century. This will be a cause for disagreement among brethren, but there is no reason why such differences cannot be resolved, provided all of the Scriptures are taken into account.

---

[1] If there is disobedience in a person's life, then ecclesial discipline may become *relevant* to that person (Matt 18 envisages a preliminary stage); once this has been determined, the discipline should be *fitted* to the situation.
[2] By this I mean just that the action is described as applying to a *kind* of individual (2 Jn v 10, Tit 3:10, 1 Tim 6:3, 2 Thess 3:6, 2 Cor 2:6). For example, elders are to be reproved (1 Tim 5:20), as were those who contradicted (Tit 1:10).
[3] Beseeching, exhortation and warning are actions directed to both individuals and larger groups.

Logic and Emotion

Brethren have always disagreed on the subject of how to tackle fellowship problems. When trouble has arisen in an ecclesia, this has often led to a localised division, or sometimes a more widespread division. Why do brethren disagree and why do they see the answer to such disagreement in division?

- Is it a matter of each person's sensitivities (emotions) on matters that makes him or her take one line?

- Is it a matter of cold logic and hard fact that brethren disagree? Is it all cut and dried?

In this section I want to conduct an examination of the *logic and emotion* of fellowship arguments. Just as most of us use the English language without any knowledge of its principles, so too most of us argue about the Bible without reflecting upon *how* we actually go about this process. Now I want to think about *how* we as a community interpret the Bible on this subject.

Interpretation and significance

Our use of language is a success story. We talk with each other using language, and we succeed most of the time. Accordingly, there is no reason to suppose that God cannot successfully communicate to us his requirements on fellowship. We mean what we say, and say what we mean, and there is no reason to suppose that this isn't true of God on the topic of fellowship. He means what He has said, and He has said what He means.

Of course, men disagree on what something means. However, this just implies that some people get it wrong.[1] This is what **interpretation** is all about: we seek to unravel the meaning of the Bible. Besides this, we also seek to know the **significance** of what we find in the Bible *for our own lives*. The significance of a passage is not just its

---

[1] A common reaction of the sceptic is to say that you can make the Bible mean anything, and his evidence is that there are dozens of views about the Bible. However, the sceptic overlooks the fact that a true view may have many competing false views.

interpretation; it is also *how the passage affects us*. When we start thinking about how a passage *affects us*, our emotions become involved.

Disagreement about fellowship then is of two broad kinds:

- disagreement about the significance of a passage - its impact on us

- disagreement over the interpretation of that passage - its intrinsic meaning

We have to keep this distinction firmly in mind. It's one thing to disagree over the 'facts', and it is another to disagree about *how the facts affect us*. We should be able to agree about the facts, but whether we can agree about how the facts affect us, this is another matter.

Interpreting the Bible
Disagreements over facts can emerge in the following way:

i) Statements might be made that generalise[1] particular examples and in this process crucial distinctions might be overlooked.[2] For example, it is only sensible to recognise that different Greek words are used in those passages that might be labelled the "withdrawal" passages (1 Cor 5, 2 Thess 3, Tit 1&2, 1 Tim 1, 6, 2 Jn v10), but some merge these passages together and make them *say the same thing*. We must resist the temptation to *conflate* the passages and make them refer to *the same kind of action*.[3] All these passages are different.

---

[1] Some people think in abstract terms, for example, it might be said that all wrong behaviour is disorderly and requires withdrawal; but the Scriptures are seldom abstract and general - in fact the fellowship data we have is wholly practical, consisting only of particular examples.

[2] It seems to me, having read much of the literature in the field, that this generalist approach towards fellowship is a common mistake. There is a powerful lure in a general and simple rule for all fellowship problems, but the Scriptures give us more avenues of action.

[3] This generalising tendency can be seen in the way that some texts are used in an abstract way in order to give a Scriptural foundation for block withdrawal. Those features of the texts, which we might label as their "ecclesial parochialism", are put aside. For example, the principle that one should withdraw from false teachers - is so

ii) Statements might be made that don't reflect the original N.T. Greek, e.g. some people may not know what the Greek for 'heretic' really means - it doesn't mean what an English reader normally understands by 'heretic'. It is important to get agreement upon the meaning of words.

iii) Statements might be made that get the context of a passage wrong. For example, some have interpreted 'if any man obey not our word by this epistle, note that man, and have no company with him' (2 Thess 3:14) as a distinct command about the failure to withdraw from a disorderly person (2 Thess 3:6), but this gets the context all wrong. Paul is addressing the brethren of v6 (see v13), and not talking about their failure or otherwise to withdraw from disorderly persons.

iv) Statements might be made that just assume certain things to be true. Assumptions play a crucial role in the interpretation of the bible. Most of the time they remain unexpressed. Where disagreement exists, assumptions are often responsible. Such assumptions are part of a way of thinking about an issue inherited from a tradition. Often they result from reading *into* a text what is not actually present. For example, in Matt 18 Christ concludes that an offending brother is to be "...as a heathen man and a publican" (v17) to the offended brother.[1] It is often assumed that this means excommunication, but this has nothing to do with the meaning of the text.

v) Statements might be made that don't take into account all of the evidence. We need to acknowledge that all Scripture is given for doctrine, for reproof and for training in righteousness (1 Tim 3:16), so

---

expressed that it is not made relative to individuals in local ecclesias, but it is generalised to become the principle that withdrawal is applicable to falsehood whether taught, held, or just present somewhere in a formal community. The consequence of this is that withdrawal can be carried out *en bloc* (applied to groups, whole ecclesias, groups of ecclesias and distinct fellowships). In order for this action to be justified, the individual aspect of the Scriptural withdrawal is put aside, and the target problem becomes abstract, for example, it becomes the presence of falsehood.

[1] The Greek 'let him be unto you' is singular.

we can't jettison parts of the Bible. For example, Biblical teaching on divorce is found in such places as Gen 2, Deut 24, Jer 3, Mal 3, Matt 5, Matt 19, Mk 10, Lk 16, Rms 7 and 1 Cor 7. We can't ignore any of these passages in formulating a Biblical doctrine of divorce and re-marriage.

vi) Statements might be made that embody small expositional mistakes about specific passages. For example, some say that the 'doctrine of Christ' in 2 Jn v9 is all the teaching of Christ, but it is apparent that it is teaching *about* the person of Christ. This allows us to use 2 Jn v9 as an example for other equivalent first principles.

Errors in doctrine emerge from small beginnings - a detail wrong here, or a mistake there, and a doctrine is flawed. Small errors can accumulate, and the cumulative effect is that the resulting doctrine can be seriously unbalanced and mislead people in the lives they lead. What is more, the small errors are usually hidden within the overall teaching and they can be missed altogether, with the result that a person may be *taken in* by the teaching.

Because of the above factors, fellowship questions may be presented in an unbalanced way. There are various ways a doctrine of fellowship can become unbalanced:

- serious flaws can be present in a treatment

- small mistakes can *accumulate* so that the overall view being presented becomes seriously skewed

- a view may be put forward as certain, whereas it ought to be presented as just a possible opinion

- rhetoric can get involved with the consequence that the treatment is distorted

All these *logical* observations point up how disagreement on fellowship matters is generated. However, agreement is perfectly possible; **it just requires brethren to work together in the co-operative task of producing doctrine according to the 'law and testimony'**.

Emotional Factors

Division between Christadelphian ecclesias and fellowships is a serious matter. All sorts of emotional factors combine to create this situation and prevent it being dissolved. By the phrase, 'emotional factors', I mean how we *feel*, what we *want*, and how we *run our lives*. We will now turn and explore some of these factors.

- Doctrine takes time, and time is not something that is easily given up to the task. Consequently, people can hold faulty views, because they do not take the time to search out a matter to see whether it is *thus or so*. Hence, they may separate from their brethren, or they may continue to support an existing division.

- Allied to time[1] there is desire. Individuals have to *want* to know the truth in a matter, but this desire is only one desire amongst other *competing* desires, and often the competing desires win out. So in fellowship matters, a person may desire to know what the truth of the matter is, but he also *wants* to be with a particular group.[2] This is a strong kind of desire, and it often wins the day. When it wins the day, the forces of compromise are needed to dull the inquiry into truth.

- Another factor is *relevance*. Life is very busy, and there are many things to be done both in and out of the truth. These days, practical considerations take priority, and a person's life is filled with holding down a job, or running a house and family. When this is done, the ordinary tasks and duties of ecclesial life fill any spare time. As a result, doctrinal matters can receive little attention. Such matters may be perceived as having little relevance, so existing divisions can continue to exist for years.

---

[1] Lack of time and the pressing requirements of other duties cannot be an excuse for avoiding the work of unity. This work should be given to those who have the time.

[2] A strong desire to keep the companionship of those we have grown up with, and a disregard for those whom we don't personally know, no matter how local they may be to our homes (cf. Jn 17).

- Yet again, not everyone can sort out a problem, and there is no reason to expect this of everyone. Some fellowship issues can become so convoluted,[1] that others get left behind wondering what is going on and where everything is leading. Such tend to follow those whom they think 'best know about the issue', and this is a natural reaction. Hence, leading brethren have led divisions in the past.

Besides these factors, there are some human traits to consider. Once a position has been adopted in public, a natural desire emerges to have been in the right all along, and not be proved wrong. When brethren adopt contrary views, human pride can become a major obstacle to progress. Jesus rebuked the disciples on several occasions, and no doubt this was an uncomfortable experience. Paul had to withstand Peter publicly for withdrawing his fellowship from Gentile Christians (Gal 2:11-13), and no doubt this was an uncomfortable experience for Peter. In our day we do not have apostles who can do this sort of thing, but this doesn't prevent our recognising the role that pride can play in divisions.

The emotional factors involved in division between ecclesias and fellowships are not all pulling in a negative direction. Some divisions are necessary (e.g. where there is apostasy and persistent immorality), and in such divisions emotions will play their part. For example, emotions like indignation, outrage, anger, intolerance and a desire to preserve the faith and its way of life.

In addition to this, existing divisions are not dissolved overnight, and rightly so for emotional reasons. Brethren and sisters are not just walking heads; they are involved with the truth in both their heart and their mind. Dissolving division is not just a work for intellectuals. The heart and the conscience of each brother and sister have to be taken into account. There is a need to consider the whole body of Christ in a fellowship, and we know that the body is made up of the weak and the strong. Each part of the body should exercise care for the other parts. It is essential therefore that fellowship differences are resolved with sensitivity to the needs of everyone in the body. The bonds that

---

[1] When fellowship problems become convoluted, this is a pretty good indication that division is the wrong answer.

exist in a fellowship have been built up over time and they are extremely important to nourishing of the whole body. These needs must remain paramount, and these emotional bonds are the positive sign of a healthy spirit of Christ.

Inter-ecclesial relationships are the responsibility of ecclesial elders. They must have their eye on the needs of the flock over which they have the oversight, and they must have regard to the problems that exist in the Christadelphian body including the problem of division. This problem cannot be put to one side because of the genuine needs of the fellowship, but rather it must be just one more of the tasks that ecclesial leaders take on board.

Disagreement and Conscience

Genuine and sincere disagreements exist over issues of fellowship, and brethren and sisters have different consciences about fellowship problems. This situation exists because people are at different stages in their understanding of the wisdom of God. All sorts of influences impinge on a person, and these affect the spirit of Christ in each individual. Each disciple of Christ is involved in a war between the spirit and the flesh, and each differs in their response. We should expect different consciences[1] in the body, and it is imperative that these are nurtured in the faith. The main examples of genuine disagreement in the N.T. concern the issue of meats (1 Cor 8) and Jewish sensitivities on various legal matters (Acts 15). In both cases the disagreement was handled within the church. It is surprising that the brotherhood has not more readily recognised the wisdom of handling genuine disagreement *within* the church.

Conclusion

If we want to understand what people say about fellowship, why disagreements exist, and so on, then it is possible to do so if we are careful. Any balanced doctrine of fellowship will embrace a variety of disciplinary actions. However, because of the finite nature of our minds (we forget things, make errors of logic, take up factual mistakes, misrepresent, indulge in rhetoric, etc.), miscalculations will be made. A balanced doctrine of fellowship takes time and effort to

---

[1] Of course, we have to examine ourselves for consciences can be affected by fleshly motives.

articulate and its application can be very variable. What we must work towards is progress and growth in all things towards Jesus who is the Head. We must exercise love (the cup of water) and concern towards those in the body of Christ in our local area whether they are in our fellowship or whether they are in another fellowship.

CHAPTER SIX
House Fellowships

Introduction
In this chapter, we are going to consider the organisation of ecclesias in the first century. There are three parts to this topic: the first part is about how believers gathered themselves in ecclesias; the second part is about how they apportioned their work in the church; and the third part is about how believers conducted their lives towards one another. We are not going to examine controversial issues that affect ecclesias today, for example, issues like the order of service, or the kind of hymns, or the Bible version to be used, the mode of address in prayer, *and so on* - these are all subjects for another time. We will just be looking at the structure of the first century church.

At the moment, most ecclesias are organised along democratic lines, with brethren taking the lead in most matters. The democracy of this approach is absent from the N.T., and it is not certain that it is a correct expression of N.T. principles. A democratic model, with its committees, constitutions, and balloting, doesn't appear in the N.T., but rather *the model is of elders leading through example and expositional teaching.*

What then was the organisation of the N.T. church? It's a dry subject perhaps, but it does have an impact on practical life in Christ. This is because organisation is just the way we associate, and love between us is mediated by how we relate together in our structures. Great divides, of course, impact on how we can love each other, since such divides mean that we have nothing to do with each other, and this is a *grave* consequence indeed.

The main structure for ecclesial life has to be small enough to facilitate love between us, and the N.T. model of ecclesial organisation was primarily that of *house-churches*. These units are mentioned in several places in the N.T., and our task will be to detail this evidence. Consequently, our treatment is expositional in character, rather than doctrinal in tone.

Once we have discussed ecclesial units, we can turn to the topic of leadership in the church. Here we will argue that there is a need to balance egalitarianism (everyone is equal in Christ) with the requirement for leadership in the body. Without leadership and responsibility in matters of the common faith, the danger is that we will all end up doing that which is right in our own eyes. Finally, we turn to look at the heart of the matter - the practical Christian life. We attempt to sketch how the basic Christian virtues underpin ecclesial structures.

House Fellowships
Repentance, belief, and baptism, incorporate a person into the body of Christ, which is the church.[1] The theological basis of fellowship is the Gospel of salvation through the Messiah of Israel, who can be identified as Jesus of Nazareth. Unity in and around Christ stems from the nature of the Abrahamic promises, and is therefore grounded in the Gospel. Disunity in its various forms is therefore contrary to the will and purpose of God. This unity is necessary to the growth of the church and the *working of God* in the church. Disunity is therefore contrary to the love that God has for the church.

The unity of believers is mainly expressed in a **small unit** - an ecclesial unit. However, it is also expressed in the relationships between ecclesias. Geography plays a part here, because inter-ecclesial relations are most prevalent in local areas. Nevertheless, Christadelphian ecclesias are part of a worldwide fellowship, and this latter kind of unity is mediated through travelling contacts and magazines. Our concern in this chapter is with *local ecclesias*.

The structure of the N.T. church is twofold: *City Ecclesias and House-Ecclesias*. We are familiar with city churches today, but here the surprising thing for us might be the mention of *houses*.

---

[1] I use the word 'church' and 'ecclesia' inter-changeably for stylistic reasons. The Christadelphian use of 'ecclesia' has the great benefit of distinguishing Christadelphian communities from the orthodox churches, and I would not like to see its demise.

A house-orientated structure, in which believers ministered[1] to each other's needs, was a feature of first century church life in a number of the city churches and during the entire apostolic period. The question arises as to why this house structure was thought valuable. My answer to this question is that this kind of structure *was and is* valuable for carrying out the practical Christian life of interpersonal care and love for one another.

Paul's epistles are usually addressed to city churches, and he addresses the church as a whole in these letters. Nevertheless, he sometimes mentions groups of believers within the letters, and he sometimes mentions **house-churches**. He does this in odd places such as greetings, goodbyes, entreaties and sundry exhortations. We will now briefly set out this evidence.

Rome - the capital of the Empire
The last chapter of Romans mentions a number of groups at Rome:

> "Greet Priscilla and Aquila...[greet] the church that is in their house..." Rms 16:3-5

> "Salute Asyncritus, Phlegon, Hermas, Patrobas, Hermes, and the brethren which are with them. Salute Philologus, and Julia, Nereus, and his sister, and Olympas, and all the saints which are with them." Rms 16:14-15

> "Salute them which are of Aristobulus' [household]. Greet them that be of the [household] of Narcissus, which are in the Lord." Rms 16:10-11

These passages suggest that believers were organised in Rome on a household basis. The phrases 'the brethren which are with them' and 'all the saints which are with them' imply groups meeting together as sub-groupings of the Roman church, to which the letter was

---

[1] I use the words 'minister' and 'ministry' in this chapter merely because they are the words used in the A.V. to describe service. I do not mean to imply that Christa-delphians ought to take up the ministry and have the ministers found in orthodox churches.

addressed.[1] It would seem that Rome had at least one house-church, and other house-groups.

Ephesus
If Rome were sub-divided into houses, what about the other major centres of the church?

> "The churches of Asia salute you. Aquila and Priscilla salute you much in the Lord, with the church that is in their house." 1 Cor 16:19

This verse shows that house churches existed elsewhere in the empire. Aquila and Priscilla again have a church in their house, but this time in Ephesus. We may presume that there were other house churches in Ephesus, since Paul preached there for three years. Indeed, Acts 20:20 indicates this, as it says that Paul taught both publicly and from *house to house*. In Paul's parting address to the Ephesian elders, he calls them elders of *the church* in Ephesus. This remark presupposes that the believers are one church in Ephesus, and this view should be put alongside the fact that there were house-churches in Ephesus (1 Tim 3:15, Gk: "in a house of God"). So we have found that both Rome and Ephesus had this arrangement.[2]

Jerusalem
Jerusalem was another large city with believers. Just as Paul taught from house to house in Ephesus, so too the apostles taught and broke bread from *house to house* (Acts 2:46, 5:42). This shows that the ministry of the church was significantly house-based. Accordingly, the daily provision for the widows was an house-to-house ministration (Acts

---

[1] The mention of women in these groups suggests church groupings rather than work fellowships, except in the case of the Aristobulus and Narcissus households. These were probably groupings based on a work-place, because the expression 'they that are of' is used of work groups (Phil 4:22, cf. Gal 6:10, 1 Tim 3:15, 2 Tim 4:19), whereas the genitive is used of families.
[2] In 1 Cor 4:17, Paul says that Timothy would remind the Corinthians of his manner of life which agreed with what he taught in *every church* (writing from Ephesus).

6), and the persecution of the Jerusalem church was on a house-to-house basis (Acts 8:3).

Although there is this evidence of a house structure in the Jerusalem church, there is also evidence that they met together in *one place*:

> "And great fear came upon all the church, and upon as many as heard these things...and they were all with one accord in Solomon's porch..." Acts 5:11-13[1]

It is possible to read this verse as suggesting that the Jerusalem church met in Solomon's porch, and this ties up with the information that the apostles were daily in the temple teaching and preaching (Acts 5:42).

Further support for the view that the Jerusalem church met as a whole and in houses can be found in Acts 15. Here we have a picture of the entire church coming together to consider the question of Gentile believers. The whole incident is a picture of the government of the church. The body of the church is given an opportunity to express its views, and yet the apostles and elders make the decision. This example compares with Paul calling the whole eldership of Ephesus together, and it shows that elders met together at the city level, and were jointly responsible for the church in that city.

In Jerusalem, then, it seems that the church's pattern of behaviour at times involved the whole church in the city, but more normally the church operated in houses, just as we have seen in Ephesus and Rome.

Laodicea

The Lycus valley was an area with several city churches. The letter to the Colossians mentions Laodicea:

> "Salute the brethren which are in Laodicea, and Nymphas, and the church which is in his house. And when this epistle is read among you, cause that it be read also in the church of the Laodiceans; and that ye likewise read the [epistle] from Laodicea." Col 4:15-16

---

[1] Cf. Acts 3:11 and the custom of Jesus mentioned in Jn 10:23.

This passage distinguishes the "church of the Laodiceans" who are the same group called "the brethren which are in Laodicea". They would evidently be joined from time to time by Colossian brethren, and on such an occasion, Paul advises the Colossians to read 'their' letter along with the letter that he has written to Laodicea.[1] One brother in Laodicea is mentioned specifically - Nymphas - he has a house church meeting. The letter to Laodicea has been 'lost', but some scholars think that this letter is the letter to Philemon,[2] and if this is correct, it mentions another house church in Laodicea:

> "And to [our] beloved Apphia, and Archippus our fellowsoldier, and to the church in thy house..." Phile v2

Alternatively, this house church might have been one of the ones in Colossae or another Lycus valley city.

Corinth
There is evidence that a 'two-tier' pattern in ecclesial life was also present at Corinth. Paul addresses his letters to the Corinthians - "to the *church* of God at Corinth" (1 Cor 1:2, 2 Cor 1:1). He instructs the "church" in various matters (e.g. 1 Cor 11, 14). In the letter to the Romans, which was written from Corinth, Paul includes a greeting (Rms 16:23) from Gaius, whom he describes as host to himself and the *whole* church in that place. This practise of the whole church meeting is mentioned in the letter:

> "If therefore the whole church be come together into one place and all speak in tongues..." 1 Cor 14:23

Yet Paul knows of a number of churches in Corinth, for he instructs,

---

[1] The Greek uses the preposition *ek* signalling that the Laodicean letter was 'out of' Laodicea. This indicates that Paul's letters became associated with their city recipients, so that the letters were circulated 'out of' their respective cities.
[2] This letter has close connections with the letter to the Colossians.

"Let the women keep silence in the churches..." 1 Cor 14:34, cf. v33b and see 1 Cor 7:17

Whether the whole church had "come together" in Gaius' house, or whether they had come together in each other's houses, they were meeting as 'an ecclesia'. In each other's houses they met as an ecclesia, just as much as if they had all assembled together in Gaius' house.

What was the character of these meetings? Were the meetings in Gaius' house for a special purpose, or was it just the same kind of meeting that they would have in each other's houses? Preaching was clearly a feature of their collected gatherings, as was the breaking of bread. They came together "to eat" (1 Cor 11:18, 20, 33), i.e. to break bread; but being together, their meetings were open at some point to unbelievers for preaching purposes (1 Cor 14:23ff). We might surmise an afternoon or early evening breaking bread, followed by a more open arrangement. More than this we cannot say: we cannot say that Gaius' house was used for just for preaching or just for the breaking of bread. It seems that the ecclesia came together in Gaius' house for the same reasons they gathered together in each other's houses - to break bread and preach the Gospel.

However, there is a difference to observe with regard to Corinthian meetings. Not all meetings of the brethren and sisters were meetings as 'an ecclesia', where sisters were expected to be silent. Some gatherings in their houses focussed on teaching, and sisters were allowed to speak and ask questions (1 Cor 14:35).[1] We may think of these meetings as meetings of a **house-group** rather than a house-church.

Gaius, like Erastus, was probably one of the more eminent men in Corinth. It would not be surprising that his home would be used for gatherings of the whole church. Ample space would be provided for

---

[1] The Greek of 1 Cor 14:35 mentions two types of house meeting: one takes place "in (an) ecclesia" and the other "in (a) house". The A.V. is unhelpful here because it interprets the Greek as referring to domestic homes and husbands and wives, whereas the Greek does not mention 'husbands', but rather the brethren (the 'your men') of a particular house group.

the necessary public meetings. In contrast to the facilities that Gaius could provide, the entertaining room of an average house would hold around thirty people, which suggests a possible size for the house churches. There were divisions at Corinth, and these were between rival house churches:

> "For it hath been declared to me concerning you, my brethren, by them [who are of the house] of Chloe, that there are contentions among you." 1 Cor 1:11 (cf. 1 Cor 16:17, which may give the identity of the messengers)

The Corinthian example is especially important today, because it includes information about the role of the memorial service and other types of meeting. The believers came together as 'an ecclesia' to break bread, but the necessary activities of explanation and discussion took place at other times. The point of special interest for us is that the practise of teaching and discussion that involves sisters speaking (asking questions) is excluded from the memorial meetings (1 Cor 14:34-35).[1]

Philippi
In another city, Philippi, there is evidence to suggest that the church initially met there in a house. In his letter to the Philippians, Paul reminds them that in the beginning of the Gospel, when he left Macedonia, "no church" entered into partnership with him in giving and receiving except them (Phil 4:15). Although he doesn't mention where the church met, we can surmise from the book of Acts that it was in the home of Lydia, the seller of purple. It was in her house that Paul stayed during his stay in Philippi, and it was to her that Paul and Silas returned after their imprisonment to see "the brethren" and exhort them before departing for Thessalonica (Acts 16:15,40). Whether other house churches developed, we do not know, and smaller towns may well have had only one group of Christians. What we see at Philippi is that the church used houses for meetings.

---

[1] The same restriction applies in respect of head coverings, but for different reasons set out in the memorial meeting chapter - 1 Cor 11.

Troas
Another example of a house meeting occurred at Troas. Here we read of Paul exhorting and breaking bread in the house of a believer in some upper room (Acts 20:6-8).

The churches of Galatia
A two-tier pattern of organisation can be discerned in the churches of Galatia. In the cities of Lystra, Iconium and Antioch, Paul and Barnabas confirmed and exhorted disciples. Of this work, we read that "when they had ordained them (i.e. the believers in these cities) elders in every church (in those cities)" (Acts 14:21-23), they left for home. Such a description implies the same sort of two tier structure we have found elsewhere.

Ecclesial Functions
If we find a two-tier structure in the first century church in such cities as Rome, Ephesus, Jerusalem and Corinth (as well as the mention of houses in other cities), then we can reasonably surmise that this was the widespread pattern of church organisation. How did the various ecclesias relate to each other and what did they do?

The main function of city churches was one of witness. We saw this with regard to Jerusalem, which met in Solomon's Porch (Acts 5:11-13), and I suggested that the same pattern was present in Corinth (1 Cor 14:23). With regard to house ministry, we find that this consisted in the breaking of bread and worshipping of God (Acts 2:46-47, 20:7-12), and also in prayer and teaching (Acts 12:12, 20:20, 1 Cor 14:35, Tit 1:11, Jms 5:14, 2 Jn v10). Concerning the time and frequency of such meetings, we have little information, except to observe that the first day of the week was a meeting day (1 Cor 16:2, Acts 20:20).

Such house churches were not completely autonomous units. We find this to be the case at least in Ephesus, where there was a city eldership (Acts 20). Paul's instructions to the elders at Ephesus imply that they were responsible for believers in the city. Similarly, the council meeting in Acts 15 indicates a city eldership, yet there was a house-based ministry at Jerusalem.

That eldership was an office[1] related to the city level of organisation can be inferred for Paul's instructions to Titus to ordain elders in every *city* (Tit 1:5), and from Paul's own example in Galatia (Acts 14:23). It would seem that elders were attached to particular houses. The particular criterion of an overseer is worth mentioning here:

> "For if a man know not how to rule his own house well, how can he take care of the church of God?" 1 Tim 3:5

Such then, I suggest, was the character of the ecclesial body in first century churches. Ought twentieth century believers to adopt such a structure? The present model is a hall-based model of organisation. This doesn't have to be abandoned in favour of a march to each other's houses, but it could be supplemented by household ministry. If there was a two-tier pattern in the first century church, each city church could own or hire a hall for general larger meetings, for preaching, for fraternals, and such like, while the basic everyday ministry of the ecclesia was carried out in houses. Two motives might be offered for adopting such an approach: one would be a desire to reflect the spiritual pattern of the N.T. church; a second would be a conviction that love and growth is best served in small informal household gatherings.

Leadership and Service in Ecclesias[2]

The purpose of life in Christ is to grow in the faith so that our lives come more and more into line with the things of God, and to this end, an important aspect of ecclesial life is leadership and inter-ecclesial leadership. (Democracy, of course, critically affects the strength of leadership).

Anglican churches have 'bishops and deacons', but these official positions bear little resemblance to the N.T. 'deacon' or 'bishop'. Paul

---

[1] The word 'office' doesn't convey anything official; it is rather a position of service.
[2] Because I am using the A.V., my terminology is correspondingly affected - I talk of bishops and deacons, but I do not intend to import into my discussion the orthodox views on these titles, neither do I think that they have any merit today.

distinguishes bishops (a better word would be 'elder' or 'overseer') and deacons (a better word would be 'servant') when he greets the Philippians:

> "Paul and Timothy, the servants of Jesus Christ, to all the saints in Christ Jesus who are at Philippi, with the bishops and deacons" Phil 1:1

And this distinction runs through the N.T. letters. For example, in 1 Tim 3, we have lists of selection criteria for bishops and deacons, and there is another list in Titus 1.

The N.T. model of ecclesial direction does not seem to be democracy and its trappings (ballots, business meetings, committees etc.),[1] for nowhere is there described such machinery. Rather, the model is one of elders and servants *appointed* by leaders (cf. Tit 1:5). Sometimes this takes place according to the wishes of an ecclesia, in other cases the appointment is by apostles. In both cases the principle of selection is a common application of certain criteria, rather than a secret ballot.

Appointment by criteria is the N.T. model.[2] Paul and Barnabas appointed elders in their city churches, and Paul passed down this practice to his retainers, Titus and Timothy, when he gave them specific lists of qualities to look for in those who would lead the ecclesia.

> "And let these also[3] first be proved; then let them use the office of a deacon, being [found] blameless." 1 Tim 3:10

> "For this cause I left thee in Crete, that thou shouldest set in order the things that are wanting, and ordain

---

[1] The current democratic structure of ecclesias seems to owe much to the prevailing business philosophy of nineteenth-century England.
[2] The apostolic example was meant to be communicated to the overseers of the churches (1 Tim 4:12, 15, cf. Phil 3:17).
[3] This remark applies to criteria for deacons, but the presence of this word 'also' means that the criteria for bishops was just as binding in their selection procedure.

elders in every city, as I had appointed thee. If any be [etc.]." Tit 1:5

The list of qualities given to Titus and Timothy is fairly lengthy, quite specific and very personal. Paul states that in selecting believers for a role, all factors must be taken into account. No role for the body of the ecclesia in mentioned in the instructions, but the examples of Acts 1 and Acts 6 show that this is not out of place. The ecclesia selected candidates collectively according to criteria, and then ecclesial leaders made the appointment.

Deacons and Servants

The A.V. word *deacon* is an anglicized translation of the Greek word *diakonos*. In Paul's epistles, there are two distinct uses of the word:

i) those believers who serve the Gospel of Christ

> "Who then is Paul, and who is Apollos, but ministers (Gk: diakonos) by whom you believed..." 1 Cor 3:5 [1]

ii) those believers who were servants of the church of which they were members

> "I commend unto you, Phoebe, our sister, which is a servant of the church which is at Cenchrea" Rms 16:1 [2]

A related word to *diakonos* is *diakonia*, and this is translated in the A.V. as 'ministry', 'administration' and 'service'. As with *diakonos* there is a similar distinction of use:

i) there is the apostolic ministry. Peter clearly had a concept of an apostolic ministry of which there were originally twelve members (Acts 1:17, 25, 6:4). Paul also had a concept of an apostolic ministry given to him (Acts 20:24). [3]

---

[1] See 2 Cor 3:6, 6:4, 11:15,23, Eph 3:7, 6:21, Col 1:7, 23-25, 4:7, 1 Thess 3:2.
[2] See Phil 1:1, 1 Tim 3:8-12, 4:6.
[3] See Acts 21:19, Rms 11:13, 2 Cor 3:8, 4:1, 5:18, 6:3, Gal 2:8, Col 4:17, 1 Tim 1:12.

ii) there were also other ministries in the church (Rms 12:6-8, 1 Cor 12:4-6, Eph 4:11-12, 1 Pet 4:10-11), grounded in the operation of the Spirit of God.[1]

The spirit-gifts are not in evidence to today, but this doesn't mean we cannot learn for the operation of the gifts in the first century, since these gifts were used to build up the ecclesia. The whole range of the gifts should be regarded as a main part of the ministry (*diakonia*) of the early church (1 Cor 12:5, Eph 4:12), but we shouldn't overlook the fact that one of the gifts was itself a distinctive gift of service (*diakonia*) in the church (Rms 12:7, 1 Pet 4:10-11).

The qualities that a servant (deacon) of the church must have are laid out in Paul's first letter to Timothy:

> "Likewise [must] the deacons [be] grave, not double tongued, not given to much wine, not greedy for money; Holding the mystery of the faith in a pure conscience. And let these also first be proved; then let them use the office of a deacon, being [found] blameless ...Let the deacons be the husbands of one wife, ruling their children and their own houses well. For they that have used the office of a deacon well, purchase to themselves a good standing, and great boldness in the faith which is in Christ Jesus." 1 Tim 3:8-13

These criteria are important, because they are a guide to us when we select those who serve in the ecclesia. In the first century, such servants may have had a spirit gift, perhaps the spirit gift of service, but we cannot be certain.

Acts 6
This chapter provides an instructive example of service in the ecclesia, and here are some of the key features:

---

[1] See Acts 6:1, 11:29, 12:25, Rms 15:31, 1 Cor 16:15, 2 Cor 8:4, 9:1ff, 2 Tim 4:5.

i) There was a physical need (the requirements of widows), but there was the 'political' relationships in the ecclesia to take into account - the relationship between Jews and Greeks.

ii) Although the need was material, the choice of *men* was based on certain spiritual qualifications (full of the spirit and wisdom, with a good reputation), qualities that the people themselves would recognise, and **by which** they were to select them.

iii) They were *appointed* by the church *leaders* - the apostles, who responsible for such matters, with the laying on of hands.

iv) An objective of the work was to *support the work of preaching*.

Perhaps the most striking difference between this example and current practice is that servants were appointed by leaders after being selected by the ecclesia according to certain criteria.

Spirit Gifts
The spirit gifts provided various functions in the early church: there were evangelists, prophets, miracle workers, healers, administrators, linguists, and helpers (1 Cor 12). It seems that the Holy Spirit "came upon" the believers or was "given" to them (Acts 8:19, 19:6), and as a result (1 Cor 12:1ff) they manifested "spiritual things", "gifts", "services" or "operations". It seems further that the Holy Spirit was ministered unto believers by someone (Gal 3:2,5) through the laying on of hands (Acts 6:6, 8:14-21, 9:17, 13:3, 19:6, cf. Acts 28:8; 1 Tim 4:14, 5:22, 2 Tim 1:6, or in direct theophany (Acts 1:10, 4:8, 10:44, 11:15). The direct bestowals of the Holy Spirit are described as 'baptisms', whereas the communication of the Spirit through the laying on of hands is never described as a baptism.

The appointment to some work is a prominent feature of the laying on of hands. For example, the apostles appointed seven to attend to the needs of widows (Acts 6); the Antiochean prophets and teachers appointed Paul and Barnabas to missionary work (Acts 13); and Timothy was appointed to the work of eldership at Ephesus (2 Tim 1). The laying on of hands and the bestowal of a spirit gift was not a widespread remit since, for example, Simon Magus and Philip weren't able to bestow the Holy Spirit in this way, and it is an attractive suggestion that it was just the apostles and elders who had this authority.

It seems probable that the gifts were widespread and available to all (1 Cor 12:31), with everyone having some gift with which to minister to the body (Rms 12:6, 1 Cor 7:7, 12:7, 1 Pet 4:10). Not all were apostles or teachers or prophets (1 Cor 12:29-30, cf. Eph 4:11), but each had a different gift, and perhaps more than one gift, according to the grace given to them (Rms 12:6, 1 Pet 4:10). In this way the Spirit divided severally to every man according to the purpose of God in building up the church (1 Cor 12:7, 11). It may be that the gifts were also available in response to earnest prayer motivated by strong desire (1 Cor 12:31, 14:1), with a view to edifying the church (1 Cor 14:12).

Twentieth Century Application

The spirit gifts have been withdrawn,[1] but God has not abandoned the work of building the church. The functions provided through the spirit gifts are just as vital today, except that the tool with which we have to work is the written word (2 Tim 3:16). The spirit-gift aims of edification and perfection of the body are just as necessary (Eph 4:11-16), and Scripture parallels the gifts in supplying us with the resources we need for growth towards these objectives.

A pastor is particularly concerned with guidance, and Scripture is profitable for instruction in righteousness; a teacher teaches doctrine, and Scripture is profitable for doctrine; a prophet would engage in reproof and correction, and this is also a function of Scripture. The aim of Scripture and the spirit gifts was the same: that a man (the body) might be perfect, thoroughly furnished for good works.

In the same way, the procedure of laying on of hands to appoint people to specific work (imparting a gift) is not practised today, but this doesn't mean we do not need servants in the ecclesia. The purpose of servants in the first century is just as valid today. We

---

[1] The proof of this cannot be undertaken here, but in summary, the "last days" bestowal of the Spirit prophesied in Isaiah and Joel was for the purpose of preaching in the last days of the Jewish Commonwealth. When this came to an end in AD70, the gifts were withdrawn.

should therefore have those who are *recognised* as serving in a specific capacity.[1]

Our main class of servant today is administrative - these are arranging brethren. Their duties include much administration. We also have exhorting brethren and teachers. Other kinds of servant include those who carry out welfare or pastoral care - the 'helpers' in Biblical terminology. We also have preachers or evangelists.

We have then a fairly well developed servant structure in the body. It is important that everyone have some role, for everyone has a part in the body. It's not possible to be a part of a body and have no function. It's not possible to be an appendix (?), you have to be at least a fingernail (Rms 12:4ff). We must have an "all member" ministry. We can't allow some members to have no purpose in the body. We will now turn and consider 'bishops' (or 'elders') and their main functions, which involved exhortation and teaching.

Bishops and Elders
The apostle Peter clarifies the role of 'bishops':

> "The elders who are among you I exhort...Feed the flock of God which is among you, taking the oversight [of it], not by constraint, but willingly; not for dishonest gain, but from a ready mind; Neither as being lords over [God's] heritage, but being examples to the flock. And when the chief Shepherd shall appear, ye shall receive a crown of glory that fadeth not away." 1 Pet 5:1-4

The work of an elder was the feeding of the flock, they were like shepherds under Christ who was the chief shepherd. Their role is described as 'oversight' (Gk: *episkopeo*). This word is used elsewhere

---

[1] Someone might argue that we can't have 'apostles' or 'miracle-workers' or 'prophets' today. We don't have these gifts, but we do have those who establish churches, which was an *apostolic* function (Eph 2:20), and we do have those who exhort and edify, which was a *prophetic* function (1 Cor 14:3, 31).

only once where it carries the sense of *looking diligently* (Hebs 12:15[1]), so elders in an ecclesia should look diligently over the flock. The associated noun to *episkopeo* is *episkopos*, and it is usually translated 'bishop' or 'overseer', so elders are overseers.

The first epistle of Peter is not the only place where we find the ideas of eldership, oversight and pastoral care combined. Consider Paul's Ephesian address:

> "Take heed therefore to yourselves, and to all the flock, over which the Holy Spirit[2] hath made you overseers, to feed the church of God, which he hath purchased with his own blood." Acts 20:28

Paul addresses this remark to the Ephesian *elders*, and he describes their work as 'oversight' again using the metaphor of the flock.[3]

The fact that elders are 'bishops' is presupposed in the instructions that Paul gives to Titus:

> "For this cause I left thee in Crete, that thou shouldest set in order the things that are wanting, and ordain elders in every city, as I had appointed thee: If any is blameless ...[etc.]...For a bishop must be blameless..." Tit 1:5-7 cf. Acts 14:23

It was the practice of Paul and his retainers to appoint elders in the city churches that they established. The use of the word 'elder' might suggest that such men were older. Indeed, Paul seems to imply that elders were to be regarded as fathers in the ecclesia to the younger brethren (1 Tim 5:1, cf. 1 Tim 3:4).

The role of an elder was that of a shepherd. This is a metaphorical description, so what does it mean? In Acts 20:28-30, there is the

---

[1] The Hebrews context can usefully be read as one addressed to elders.
[2] That is, the Holy Spirit working through Paul, hence Ananias and Sapphira lie to the Holy Spirit in Peter.
[3] Again, consider the title that Peter ascribes to Christ - "Shepherd and Bishop" - mixing pastoral care of a flock with oversight.

aspect of the *protection* of the flock against those who speak perverse things. Such a responsibility devolves upon those most able to deal with such people, viz. elders. It would be odd indeed if the sheep were to take on the wolves![1]

Elders then are *responsible* for the flock, but they are not to dominate it, rather they are to be examples to the sheep. Elders then have a certain *authority* (1 Pet 1:1-3). Accordingly, there is to be reciprocal obedience and submission by the flock (Hebs 13:7, 17, 24).[2]

The idea of *rulership* can conjure up images of dictatorship, or images of 'clergy and laity'. These institutions illustrate the love of power, but the rulership in the ecclesia should always be a matter of *guidance*:

> "Let the elders that rule [3] well be counted worthy of double honour, especially they who labour in the word and doctrine." 1 Tim 5:17
>
> "...he that ruleth, with diligence; he that sheweth mercy, with cheerfulness." Rms 12:8
>
> "A bishop then must be... One that ruleth well his own house, having his children in subjection with all gravity; (For if a man knoweth not how to rule his own house, how shall he take care of the church of God?)" 1 Tim 3:2f

---

[1] The large amount of detail presented on issues of protective and corrective care (in this series) should illustrate the importance that attaches to such actions.

[2] The Greek verb involved in these Hebrews verses is *egeomai* (them which have the rule over you). It can carry the sense of 'lead' (Acts 15:22, 22:24), 'govern' (Acts 7:10), and 'rule' (Matt 2:6). These latter two uses are political uses, while the first use is that of exercising leadership in a more general sense. According to these verses in Hebrews, such leaders we are to obey (cf. 1 Pet 5:5), follow their faith (cf. 1 Cor 1:11), and consider their way of life.

[3] The Greek verb in these verses is *proistemi* and it is best understood in the reference to a man ruling his own house.

> "And we beseech you, brethren, to know them who labour among you, and are over you in the Lord, and admonish you;" 1 Thess 5:12-13a

Elders taught, i.e. they *fed* the flock (they therefore needed to be apt to teach), but only *some of them* did this task (1 Tim 5:17). This ties in with our suggestion that the functions of eldership were shared among several elders (cf. 1 Tim 4:14, Jms 5:14).

> "For a bishop must be blameless...Holding fast the faithful word as he hath been taught, that he may be able by sound doctrine to exhort and to convict [those who] contradict." Tit 1:7-9

Elders also *exhorted* with sound doctrine and reproved those who contradicted. The council decision of the apostles and elders described in Acts 15 is an example of explicit and binding doctrinal guidance.

Elders gave direction and guidance, and this involved *correction* from time to time.[12] Warning and admonishment were daily functions of ecclesial elders, and closely associated with teaching. Paul's example was to warn on a daily basis, and he commends his example to the Ephesian elders (Acts 20:30). In 1 Thess 5:14, Paul exhorts 'the brethren' to warn those who are unruly. These 'brethren' are those who are 'over' the others 'in the Lord' (1 Thess 5:12) and who exercise the function of admonishment. (1 Cor 4:14-15a, 2 Thess 3:15). Such admonishment is not a "telling off" but a particular kind of targeted teaching (Col 1:28), intended to change behaviour and perfect believers (cf. Eph 4:12). Elders were also responsible for matters of *welfare* (Acts 20:34-35). They were to take *care* of the church (1 Tim 3:2f). It is the same idea of care that we find in the parable of the Good Samaritan. Such care is a practical care for the material needs of the church, and this duty fits the picture of elders as fathers

---

[1] Paul in Hebs 12:15ff exhorts that oversight be directed towards i) stopping believers falling from grace; ii) preventing the roots of bitterness springing up thereby defiling others; iii) preventing fornications and profanities in the ecclesia.

[2] We examined ecclesial discipline in Chapter 5.

in the ecclesia (cf. Acts 6). We can summarise the functions of elders as follows:

- to teach the Word of God through exposition and exhortation

- to exercise the authority inherent in their position of oversight, for example, with regard to correction

- to protect the flock against false teachers

- to care for the welfare needs of the flock

It seems to me that ecclesias need leadership and direction given by a body of elders, appointed according to Biblical criteria. Such would be responsible for overall spiritual and material welfare, with particular responsibility for doctrine and exhortation, correction and protection. Supplementing their work, with the work of service, there will be those who are recognised to be servants of the ecclesia.

It's all a matter of balance. Ecclesias are presently run on egalitarian, voluntarist and democratic principles. The role of an 'elder' hasn't really been particularly emphasized, except in perhaps the 'wise old man' sense. There is a need to re-dress the balance and introduce greater recognition of the role of 'elders' in the N.T. church, and recognise elders in each ecclesia. Such elders would be associated with house-churches in the first instance, but they would co-operate with other elders from other house churches in the city to organise city wide preaching and fraternal events. There is just as much need for inter-ecclesial leadership as there is for ecclesial leadership, and this is primarily facilitated through the contacts that elders develop.

One Another Virtues

What is the Christian life? We have provided glimpses of one picture in our description of house-churches and the role of servants and elders, but the glimpses have been of just the outward forms of the body. We need to tackle the heart of Christian life itself, not the individual life, but the ecclesial life.

Christian life in the ecclesia is essentially a life of one anotherness - hence, the church is a *body*. The N.T. mentions various "one another" virtues,[1] which are to pervade inter-personal relationships in the ecclesia. The pattern for us to follow is set down by Paul:

> "So we, being many, are one body in Christ, and every one members of another" Rms 12:5

This point is the fundamental conditioning factor of ecclesial life. It indicates a high level of involvement with others in our ecclesia, and it is essentially the requirement that we should *love one another*.

A small house fellowship would have been a structure that was informal, intimate and flexible, and these are the very qualities that are essential to loving one another. If we are to love one another, we have to *know* one another, and a smaller group is the only practical way that this can be achieved. Not only this, we cannot love everyone, for we are limited by circumstances - it seems we can only love a small number of people - and so a smaller group would be the natural vehicle for exercising the care that we should have for one another.

My suggestion is that our organisational structures should emerge from the Christian life, rather than be imposed upon us as a straitjacket. We might enter an ecclesia, and it may have existing ways of doing things, but these ways should reflect the Christian life - they should have emerged from the practise of the commands of Christ. When I talk of 'structure' (house churches), I do not have something formal and institutional in mind, when I talk of deacons (servants) or bishops (elders) I do not have formal 'offices' in mind. Instead, I am just trying to convey, in an imperfect way, some sense of how believers practised the ordinary daily ecclesial life.[2] The words we use to describe our communal structures don't matter so much as the underlying practise of the Christian life. It is this life that matters, and this is why fellowship matters, because the Christian life is a life of fellowship in one body. Thus, although this chapter might appear to be a dry intellectual exercise at times, its objective is wholly practical.

---

[1] That is, identifiable by the phrase 'one another', 'one to another' and 'each other'.
[2] The first century ecclesial life was a *daily* affair, rather than an institutional once a week Sunday visit.

Love is the "tying bond" of perfection (Col 3:14, cf. 2:19); and peace is the "tying bond" (Eph 4:3) of fellowship. But love is not something vague or abstract, neither is it something we applaud like motherhood or apple pie, but rather it is seen in and through various ways of behaving - behaviour such as kindness, deference, mercy, patience, forbearance and forgiveness. The practise of these qualities *creates* fellowship. One such list would include the following:

> "[Be] kindly affectioned one to another with brotherly love; in honour preferring one another..." Rms 12:10

> "And be ye kind one to another, tenderhearted, forgiving one another..." Eph 4:32

> "...in lowliness of mind let each esteem others better than themselves. Look not every man on his own things, but every man also on the things of others." Phil 2:3b-4, cf. 1 Cor 10:24, 1 Tim 5:21

> "...no schism in the body; but...the members should have the same care one for another." 1 Cor 12:25

> "Bear ye one another's burdens..." Gal 6:2, cf. Rms 15:1
> "And let us consider one another to stir up to love and to good works..." Hebs 10:24

> "Use hospitality one to another without grudging..." 1 Pet 4:9

> "Submitting yourselves one to another in the fear of God." Eph 5:21, cf. 1 Pet 5:5

> "Confess [your] faults one to another, and pray one for another..." Jms 5:16, cf. Gal 6:1

> Put on therefore, as the elect of God, holy and beloved, tender mercies, kindness, humbleness of mind, meekness, longsuffering; Forbearing one

> another, and forgiving one another..." Col 3:12-13, cf. Eph 4:2

> "Praying always with all prayer and supplication in the Spirit, and watching for this purpose with all perseverance and supplication for all saints;" Eph 6:18

> "And I myself also am persuaded concerning you, my brethren, that ye also are full of goodness, filled with all knowledge, able also to admonish one another." Rms 15:14

> "For, brethren, ye have been called to liberty; only [use] not liberty for an occasion to the flesh, but by love serve one another." Gal 5:13

> "Let us therefore follow after the things which make for peace, and things with which one may edify another." Rms 14:19, cf. v2

> "Wherefore comfort one another with these words. " 1 Thess 4:18, cf. Hebs 3:13

> "Let the word of Christ dwell in you richly in all wisdom; teaching and admonishing one another in psalms and hymns and spiritual songs, singing with grace in your hearts to the Lord." Col 3:16, cf. Eph 5:19

Apart from these virtues, to which no doubt others could be added, love is the most often mentioned one another virtue:[1]

> "But concerning brotherly love ye need not that I write to you: for ye yourselves are taught by God to love one another." 1 Thess 4:9

> "For this is the message that ye have heard from the beginning, that we should love one another." 1 Jn 3:11

---

[1] See also Rms 13:8, 2 Thess 1:3, 1 Pet 2:22, 1 Jn 3:23, 4:7, 11, 12.

> "And above all things have fervent charity among yourselves: for charity shall cover a multitude of sins." 1 Pet 4:8

> "And the Lord make you to increase and abound in love one toward another..." 1 Thess 3:12

Our love is to *increase* and *abound* towards one another; we are to have *fervent* love among us. In other words, a static, passive love (a mere attitude of mind) is not real Christian love. Such a love would not be involved with others. By contrast, the presence of active love will create active patterns of behaviour - structures - in the ecclesia. Let us group these 'one another' virtues.

Getting involved is a risk. You risk getting hurt. It involves confidence and trust. One involving virtue is the riskiest of all: *Confess your faults to one another,*[1] *and pray for one another.* Such confession would exemplify openness towards one another, and our mutual caring for one another would thereby be enriched. A related virtue is: *And let us consider one another to provoke unto love and good works.* This virtue could be achieved in and through counselling structures in the church, since the purpose of Christian counselling is to consider others and provoke them unto good works and away from sin. Clearly, confession of sin and counselling imply a fair degree of personal involvement in the lives of each other. In Gal 6:1, we read of another counselling virtue: *if a man be overtaken in a fault, ye which are spiritual restore such a one.* Notice that this virtue is restricted to those who are spiritual, so maybe only these need to know about faults. Such a facility, if it existed, would enable believers to bear one another's burdens.

Interest in one another's well being, and involvement in each other's lives is a Scriptural requirement, it has nothing to do with being a nosy busybody. We are to be equally concerned for all parts of the body of Christ, and we should structure and pattern our ecclesial lives to ensure that this inter-personal care is facilitated.

---

[1] I do not suggest the introduction of priests here, but rather a more frank and open consideration of the sins that do so easily beset us and how we can best overcome them.

Other virtues that we listed above might be called 'serving virtues'. Believers are to build one another up, teach one another, admonish one another and exhort one another. These virtues exist because there is meant to be growth in the body of Christ towards perfection. It is because of this need that there are elders and servants.

Perfection, in the sense of maturity, is a goal of Christian life. This is the purpose of service in the ecclesia (Eph 4:13, cf. Col 1:28, 4:12). In particular, Paul is concerned with the 'perfection' of understanding (Hebs 5:14, 6:1, cf. Phil 3:15). Elsewhere, the concept of perfection (Gk: *teleios*) is associated with the full knowledge to be gained from the Scriptures (1 Cor 13:10) and, hence, Paul exhorts the Corinthians to be perfect in understanding (1 Cor 14:20). More generally, the apostles express their desire for growth, not only in knowledge, but also in matters of behaviour.

Conclusion

By reflecting on the practical virtues of the Christian life, we can see that they are the heart of fellowship. At the end of the day, fellowship is not a formal matter, but a living and involving experience. It is from the practice of Christian virtue that real fellowship emerges. Such fellowship will be readily identifiable in the way we relate to one another - in our structures. In this book we have sought to identify patterns of behaviour, patterns of leadership and patterns of ecclesial grouping that naturally emerge from the practise of the virtues of the Christian life. In conclusion, they are why *fellowship matters*.

Appendix

Repentance, Forbearance and Marriage Problems

Introduction
In this appendix, I want to look at the topics of marital failure, repentance and forbearance. I want to consider God's forgiveness and His mercy. I also want to examine how ecclesias should treat cases of divorce and re-marriage. There are many treatments on the topic of marriage and divorce, and this appendix is not a full length study of Bible teaching on the subject. In any event, there is very little to add *pro and con* to the material that *already* exists. So our study is by way of an evaluation and overview of the arguments and presentation of a straightforward conclusion.

In the Bible we are presented with two sides to the character of God: He is on the one hand a merciful God, and yet on the other He is a God of judgement. He has laid down standards of behaviour, and the punishment for disobedience is death. The exercise of His righteous judgement can lead to only one sentence, but the exercise of His mercy leads to the bestowal of life. In fellowship terms, *we* have the same choice - to exercise judgment and apply ecclesial discipline, or to forbear, exercise patience and accept imperfection.

The children of God have to imitate His example; they have to exercise judgment and apply discipline in the ecclesia, but they also have to exercise longsuffering and forbearance of one another, seeking in each other the confession of sin and repentance. The practise of these things is difficult, and a cause for disagreement among brethren and sisters across all fellowships and ecclesias. Disagreement in this area has led to division of groups of ecclesias; it has led to a breakdown of relations between ecclesias in a fellowship. Should disagreement about marriage and divorce divide groups of ecclesias? There are two steps to an answer. Step one sets down the

Biblical *data* on divorce and re-marriage, and step two addresses the problem of disagreement between brethren and sisters. The first step involves Bible exposition, and here the problem is how to understand Deuteronomy 24 and Genesis 2. The second step is about what policy we should have towards each other when we disagree on this question.

If there is a difference of view, should this difference be handled through the device of a 'new church', a new autonomous fellowship? Or should the differences be handled through the device of local ecclesial autonomy? Should the conscience of brethren and sisters be handled within the body in separate ecclesias, or should the conscience of brethren and sisters be handled by setting up a new and *competing* church? Any writer who writes on the topic of Christadelphian fellowship has to consider divorce and re-marriage and he has to address these questions.

The question of divorce and re-marriage has dominated many discussions of fellowship. The ideal standard is not questioned. All parties accept that marriage was intended to be for life. But what if there is a divorce (and re-marriage), what should be our attitude? Can we allow different attitudes to divorce to prevail amongst ecclesias? Or should all ecclesias practise one policy? Is a policy on divorce part of the *basis of fellowship* for all ecclesias? The Biblical texts are well known, and the various approaches to these texts are well known. We shall start with the Law of Moses, proceed to the Prophets, and then turn to the teaching of Christ and Paul.

The Law of Moses
The Law of Moses begins with Genesis. There the pattern is laid down: one man and one woman for life (Matt 19:3ff). There is no doubt about this principle. A person is married, according to Genesis, when he leaves his mother and father and cleaves to a woman who is thereby **made** his wife. It's irrelevant to this definition of marriage whether a marriage is ratified on paper by the state. A marriage consists of commitment and sexual union. It has a spiritual dimension as well as a physical. Eve was created as a 'helpmeet' for Adam. [11]

---

[1] Some think that Genesis is about stories and not part of the Law. But in the case of the creation of Adam and Eve, it is the Mosaic

The Fall occurred, and man became subject to sin and death. The fact that the standard was laid down *before* the Fall is significant. This is all too often overlooked. Adam and Eve were brought together when creation was very good. We can only surmise about their relationship before the Fall. There must have been a very real sense of empathy between the pair, because they were literally 'bone of bone' and 'flesh of flesh'. But then a curse was laid upon man, and marriage since then has been a pale copy of the ideal. The relationship of Adam and Eve was changed - 'your desire shall be to your husband, and he shall rule over thee'. The effects of the curse must have taken their toll on Adam and Eve's marriage. But the ideal of their marriage before the Fall will again be seen in the marriage of Christ and his bride.

The history of marriage since the Fall has been one where the standard was often breached. Here it has to be accepted that polygamy and the taking of concubines (by great men of faith, e.g. 2 Sam 12:8) are as much a breach of the Genesis standard as any divorce and re-marriage, although God doesn't say that He hates polygamy while He does say that He hates divorce (Mal 2:16). It's too easy to turn a blind eye to this fact of Biblical history. Why were the great men of faith not required to maintain the 'one man one woman' principle?

It's essential to lay down the law on divorce. To get a divorce is contrary to the Genesis command. And the seriousness of divorce can be seen when the typology of marriage is borne in mind. The relationship between a man and a wife is meant to reflect the future relationship between Christ and the bride. This is not just an optional lifestyle. If a person gets a divorce, they destroy this typology in their lives.

---

narrator who stipulates the principle "Therefore shall a man leave his father and his mother, and shall cleave unto his wife: and they shall be one flesh". These are not Adam's words, since he had no mother or father! Hence Jesus directs the Pharisees - 'have ye not read?' (Matt 19:4), and Paul can observe that 'the wife is bound (cleaved) by the **law** to her husband as long as her husband liveth' (1 Cor 7:39).
[1] Hence, in the Law, when an unbetrothed virgin was humbled, the man had to marry her (Ex 22:16, Deut 22:28).

The Genesis standard is not a *law* forbidding forms of behaviour, but rather, it is a standard tied to the creation of male and female. But the Law of Moses does have *laws* about marriage, and about the Jewish betrothal period, which was the time when couples were engaged to be married:

- adultery with another man's wife required the sentence of death (Lev 20:10).[1]

- sex before marriage by a 'virgin' was a capital crime (Deut 22:13-21).[2] If the man's accusation of such behaviour was wrong, he was forbidden to get a divorce (Deut 22:19).

- a betrothed virgin found in the sex act with a man in a city was to be stoned (Deut 22:24-25), but not if she were found in the countryside.[3]

- in the case of sex before marriage between those who were *not* betrothed, the man was to marry the virgin and he was forbidden to get a divorce (Ex 22:16-17, Deut 22:28-29).

- the Law acknowledged divorce action by the man, and legislated for any subsequent re-marriage on the part of the woman (Deut 24:1).

But the Law doesn't supply us with any laws *about* divorce! It mentions divorce only in the framing of *other* laws. This is a key point. It mentions divorce in connection with laws about sex before marriage (Deut 22:19, 24). Because divorce is referred to in laws about sex before marriage, it would be reasonable to say that this was the only reason for which divorce was an acknowledged practise,

---

[1] The Law is framed in terms of 'the man' and a married man at that, and the Law is also framed in terms of a woman who is already a *wife* rather than a woman who is *single*.
[2] This says nothing about men being virgins on their wedding night
[3] It's not clear whether sex had to have occurred *during* betrothal, or *before*.

except that the Law also mentions divorce in the framing of a law about *re-marriage* (Deut 24:1-4). This reads as follows:

> "When a man takes a wife and marries her, and it happens that she finds no favour in his eyes because he has found some thing of nakedness in her, and he writes her a certificate of divorce, puts it in her hand, and sends her out of his house, when she has departed from his house, and goes and becomes another man's, [if] the latter husband detests her and writes her a certificate of divorce, puts it in her hand, and sends her out of his house, or if the latter husband dies who took her to be his wife, [then] her former husband..." Deut 24:1-4[1]

It's very easy to mis-read Deuteronomy 24:1-4. The passage is a set of relative clauses:

'**When** [such and such have happened]...

    and **when** [such and such have happened]...

        and **if** [there is a second divorce]...

        or **if** [the second husband dies]...

then her former husband *must not...*'

The subject matter of the regulation actually concerns the woman's relationship to the first husband in certain circumstances. The text isn't a statement *at all* of the conditions under which divorce was permissible. One circumstance is mentioned in passing, but the law is framed *about* re-marriage.

---

[1] Most versions translate Deut 24:1-4 as an extended set of relative clauses antecedent to the consequent clause about re-marriage, and contrary to the A.V., for example, NKJV, ASV, RSV, Young's Literal and Darby's Literal versions.

The central euphemism of the re-marriage law is similar but not identical to that used when describing various forms of incest in Leviticus 18. The phrase used in Lev 18 is 'the nakedness of...'. It may be that the law is framed with such incests in mind, or it may be that the euphemism, 'a matter of nakedness', is more generally referring to sexual immorality. The Hebrew phase translated 'a matter of nakedness' is *ervat davar*, and it occurs elsewhere only in Deut 23:14:

> "For the Lord thy God walketh in the midst of thy camp, to deliver thee, and to give up thine enemies before thee; therefore shall thy camp be holy: that he see no unclean thing (ervat davar) in thee, and turn away from thee" Deut 23:14

The immediate context (Deut 23:10-13, v14='for') for this use of *ervat davar* is of toiletry matters, during which nakedness occurs. So it would appear that this is a *literal* use of the expression. In this verse, 'a matter of nakedness' is associated with the Lord 'turning away' from Israel, and likewise in Deut 24:1, 'a matter of nakedness' is associated with a turning away, i.e. a divorce. This may be the reason for the use of the same phrase in both cases. A divorce is a turning away from an unclean thing which has been seen by the husband, although with a divorce the issue is not a toiletry one, as we shall see when we look at Christ's *authoritative interpretation* of Deut 24. This re-marriage law has been the subject of endless interpretation because of its central euphemism, 'a matter of nakedness'.[1] What does this mean? Three views can be considered: it has been applied to,

- sex during betrothal
- sex before betrothal
- adultery

The framing of the law has some contacts with the law covering sex before marriage (see Figure 1), and these contacts indicate that the

---

[1] Christ carried over the scope of this central euphemism when he used the word *porneia* (translated 'fornication') for the Hebrew *ervat davar* (a matter of nakedness). The Greek word is a general word for sexual immorality, rather than a specific word denoting adultery.

'matter of nakedness' has to do with some sort of sexual immorality. But is it immorality that takes place *before* or *after* marriage? Here, commentators disagree. Does Deut 24 concern women who have been put away because of adultery? The problem with this view is that adultery was a capital crime. Does Deut 24 concern women who have been put away because of sex with someone else before marriage? The problem with this comparison is that the pre-marital immorality in Deut 22 was also a capital crime. This leads to the suggestion that Deut 24 is about pre-betrothal sexual immorality and that Deut 22 is just about *betrothal immorality*.

when a man hath taken (Deut 24:1)	If any man take (Deut 22:13)
she find no favour (Deut 24:1)	And hate her (Deut 22:13)
the latter husband hate her (Deut 24:3)	
send her out (Deut 24:1)	**He may not put her away** (Deut 22:19, 29)

Figure 1: Pre-Marital Law and Divorce

This view is known as the ***pre-betrothal view of Deut 24***. It has some problems. It assumes that Deut 22 is *only* about betrothal unfaithfulness. This isn't actually stated in the text. The immorality referred to in Deut 22 might have happened *during* betrothal, but maybe it was *before* any betrothal. The guilty woman in Deut 22 is, after all, accused of prostitution (Deut 22:21), and this is surely a sin regardless of her status - betrothed or otherwise. Virginity was important in the Law, and Deut 22 is about whether a woman was a virgin on her wedding night. Another question to pose against the pre-betrothal view is that the text of the re-marriage law mentions *two divorces*, and the second divorce is a divorce of a second marriage, and it seems inappropriate to compare *this second* divorce with the law about betrothal unfaithfulness or the circumstances of a pre-betrothal period. Finally, Deut 24 doesn't seem to be about the marriage night and the tokens of virginity, because there the woman finds no favour in her husband's eyes after a period of time (i.e. *it shall come to pass*).

In the absence of a specific Mosaic divorce law, we must rely on inference as to what actually were the divorce practises of the

Israelites. The euphemism of the re-marriage law is wide enough to embrace cases of sex before marriage. Perhaps it was used in this way, and the case of Joseph and Mary would show such a use of the law. But if it were, we cannot stop at this, if only because the text of the law mentions two divorces, the last of which is a divorce of a second marriage.

All the Law allows us to say is that divorce took place for matters of nakedness, and divorce severed the marriage bond. Besides this kind of severance of the marriage bond, death, betrothal unfaithfulness and adultery[1] (both leading to execution) severed the marriage bond under the Law of Moses.

The *pre-betrothal view* assumes that the divorce practises of the nation were determined by the law of Moses. But since there was no law or set of regulations about divorce, can we make this assumption? Can we assume that an Israelite only practised divorce in those sexual circumstances when a capital crime was *not* involved? Can we assume that an Israelite upheld the law in matters of sexual immorality and only sought divorce for pre-betrothal unfaithfulness?

The re-marriage law has an ambiguous euphemism in it, and in our day and age we could look at other laws to provide a framework for interpreting the ambiguous law. But the law itself doesn't invite us to demarcate its scope in this way. Had it been a regulation stipulating the conditions of divorce, then we would have rightly interpreted it within the framework of the whole Law. But the text of the re-marriage law only refers to the *practises of the Israelites.*

What if the re-marriage law *complemented* the other laws? What if divorce were a course of action that was being taken when the other

---

[1] The only argument presented here for the view that adultery breaks the marriage bond is the fact that it was a capital crime under the Law of Moses. A person today could argue like this: my spouse has committed adultery and the Law shows that this merits death; had we been under the Law, my marriage would have been dissolved; but although adultery is not a capital crime today, surely the Law shows that I can dissolve my marriage. Such an attitude betrays a certain hardness.

fornication laws were **not** invoked? Since there were no divorce rights **in** the Law, the clause about divorce in the re-marriage law must have referred to a practise among the people, a practise running alongside the Law that the Law sought to address.

If a man were faced with the adultery of a spouse, he might choose divorce in his own case. He might not choose to invoke the law of adultery. If a man were faced with a wife who was not a virgin, he might invoke the recognition of divorce (cf. the example of Joseph) by the Law, rather than invoke the law of betrothal infidelity. These alternative actions might have been going on in the Israelite congregation, and the Law, we suggest, might be regulating for these situations.

Divorce in the Prophets

In the Law, divorce was acknowledged for 'a matter of nakedness', but this term isn't narrowly defined. In the prophets however, there is an exercise of a 'Deuteronomy style' divorce by God Himself, who gave Israel a 'bill of divorcement':

> "Thus saith the Lord, Where is the bill of your mother's divorcement, wherewith I have put her away...behold for your transgressions was your mother put away..." Is 50:1

> "I saw when, for this very cause that back-sliding Israel had committed adultery I had put her away, and given her a bill of divorcement..." Jer 3:8

> "I spread my skirt over thee...and entered a covenant with thee...and thou becamest mine...But thou...playedst the harlot...a wife that committeth adultery...I will judge thee as women that commit adultery..." Ezek 16:8-38

Because Israel had broken the covenant by committing adultery with the surrounding nations, God would treat them as women that had committed adultery, He gave them a bill of divorcement. He might have destroyed them, as the Law prescribed, but He did not do this and executed *instead* an act of divorce.

These texts establish an application of the kind of divorce acknowledged in the Law and they show that adultery can lead to a breaking of the marriage bond. Israel would have been free to marry again. But God still pleaded with her to return to Him (Jer 3:1). He was prepared to betroth her again in a fresh union. When Israel says, 'I will go and return to my first husband', then God's response is 'I will betroth thee unto me for ever' in a new covenant (Hos 2:7,11:9, Jer 31:31).

The re-marriage law of Deut 24 allowed a return to the first husband provided a second marriage had not been contracted.[1] This was the case for Israel. Although she was put away in order that she might chase 'her lovers', she did not marry false gods in her exile[2] (through any national covenant). Since her return from exile, she has not married other gods nor sought them in idolatry. The way is open for a further marriage, because she has not been defiled[3] by another man.

How is the 'Deuteronomy style' divorce applied to Israel? One suggestion is that the divorce was made because of Israel's pre-Sinai immorality (in Egypt, see Ezek 20:7-8, 23:19,27 and contrast Ezek 23:8). But Israel's behaviour in Egypt is only background reasoning. The divorce is made *for adultery*. The case of Hosea shows this to be the case: he married a whore, who then continued to be such throughout the marriage.

We saw that the central expression of the re-marriage law was 'a matter of nakedness', and the term 'nakedness' features in the prophetic description of Israel's *marital* unfaithfulness (e.g. Hos 2:9). The law of re-marriage says nothing about the 'matter of nakedness', and the euphemism '...nakedness' is used to refer to all kinds of sexual irregularity. Within the *case law* of the Law of Moses, Deut 24 has been

---

[1] There is some debate over the re-marriage law of Deut 24, and this debate concerns whether the law forbad re-marriage to a first husband altogether.

[2] Ephraim were *joined* to idols (Hos 4:17), but not married to them, because they had not yet been divorced. The expression *joined* can denote marriage, but it can also denote the unfaithfulness of a spouse, e.g. Num 25:3,5, Ps 106:28.

[3] The reference to defilement may suggest that a second marriage defiled the wife for the first husband so that he could not re-marry.

applied to the situation of the adultery of a wife. We cannot exclude this kind of application, consequently we suggest that Deut 24 embraces all kinds of sexual mal-practise such as harlotry, adultery, and pre-marital immorality.

The Teaching of Jesus

The example of God shows us that divorce breaks the marriage bond, and re-marriage is possible for the unfaithful wife. No comments are made in the prophets about the re-marriage of the husband, and God remained faithful to the miscreant wife.[1] The scope of the clause should be understood in the light of God's relationship with Israel. It is important to stress that the divorce clause does not enshrine a right, but rather it shows a practise being regulated by the Law. It shows that a concession had been made by Moses for the hardness of heart on the part of man. Jesus comments on the divorce clause in Deut 24. He reinforces what has become known as the **exceptive clause**,

> "Whosoever shall put away his wife, saving for the cause of fornication, causeth her to commit adultery…" Matt 5:32, cf. Matt 19:9

The words of Christ assume (following Deut 24) that the woman would remarry, and his comment is that she would, in certain circumstances, commit adultery. The law in Deuteronomy envisaged that the woman might remarry, though there is no *right* to re-marry.

The scope of 'fornication' embraces sexual immorality, including adultery. This is a general word, and not the specific word for adultery used in the same verse. This implies that 'a matter of nakedness' has a general application to sexual immorality. God had divorced Israel for reasons of adultery, marital unfaithfulness and harlotry.

All this, however, could be academic. It's one thing to determine what the Law of Moses meant, but does this have any relevance for *us* today? Brethren and sisters might disagree about the interpretation of Deut 24, but is this anything more than an expositional disagreement? If it is, it shouldn't be a cause for division. On the other hand can we

---

[1] It would appear from Hosea that Israel did not marry any of her adulterous lovers in her exile (Hos 2:7).

dismiss the Law? We may dismiss the ceremonial laws and the laws that are culturally relative to Israel's national life, but the moral laws and the principles illustrated by them cannot be dismissed. To be true, the text of the re-marriage law relates to another nation, and we are not *that* nation. We cannot just take the re-marriage law and apply it to our lives today. For a start, we have no legal rights to issue bills of divorce! Rather, we should look at the moral principle in the law and take our teaching from that principle.

It has been argued that Christ's commentary on the law has no application to the Christian dispensation. It has been put that Christ raised the requirements for believers to a higher level - the Edenic level. It has been suggested that elsewhere Christ pronounces upon this divorce matter without mentioning an exceptive clause (Mk 10:1-12, Lk 16:18). We must therefore examine the relationship of these other verses to the 'exceptive' clause passages.

The record in Mark is clearly an account of the incident recorded in Matthew 19, but it is an account that stresses a different part of the exchange between Jesus and the Pharisees. In the Matthew excerpt, the Pharisees ask whether it is lawful to divorce *for every cause*. Hence, Jesus defines the *one* exceptive clause in Matthew. Mark records a different part of the exchange between Jesus and the Pharisees, for in Mark's account the Pharisees ask whether divorce was lawful *at all*. So Jesus says that it is lawful *but suffered*, and Jesus makes no comment about an exceptive clause in Mark's account.

The question arises as to whether Mark's account should be seen in a different light to that of Matthew's. The exceptive clause is not mentioned and there is added detail:

> "And in the house his disciples asked him again of the same matter. And he saith unto them, Whosoever shall put away his wife, and marry another committeth adultery against her. And if a woman shall put away her husband, and be married to another, she committeth adultery." Mk 10:11-12

The added details here are: *the disciples are in a house*, and the Pharisees are *no longer present*. The disciples however are asking about the *same* matter of there being a divorce clause in the Law (Mk 10:4).

Matthew and Mark record the same exchange, which takes place in public. When we read that Jesus and his disciples have shifted to a house, and when we read that the disciples raise the same matter again, we have to take this subsequent exchange in the light of the previous public controversy with the Pharisees (*as far as we have it in Mark*). This was an exchange about *the Law of Moses*, and consequently, Jesus would still be replying in this context. This is an important point. The context of the further conversation is still the Law of Moses. It has to be remembered that Jesus' teaching was given in a Jewish framework, but this doesn't mean we can reject that teaching.

But Christ is supplying further teaching *in the house*, further teaching not covered by the divorce clause in the Law. He refers to the man divorcing and marrying again, which the re-marriage law doesn't mention, and he refers to the woman divorcing and marrying again, which is again not mentioned in this law. In making these further observations therefore Jesus is **not** commenting on Deut 24. The focus of Christ is upon *the person (man or woman) that puts asunder*, and his further remarks in the house therefore amplify his dictum 'let not man put asunder'. A person who puts asunder, and marries again, commits adultery. Christ's own inference from Genesis 2 is 'let not man put asunder',[1] and from this it follows that divorce for *any cause* leads to adultery if (an important and often overlooked *if*) there is re-marriage.

Christ gives teaching on the Law, and he defines the exceptive clause, but he also gives teaching on Genesis 2, and there is no exceptive clause in Genesis, (hence Rms 7:2, 1 Cor 7:10a, 11[b], 39). Is this contradictory? Is Genesis at variance with Deuteronomy? This is a big problem, and we can look at the two main proposals:

---

[1] The indissolubility of marriage is illustrated by a) only *one* man and *one* woman were created; b) they were to *cleave* together; c) they were *one* flesh; d) there was *no one else* with whom either could be one.

1) We can reject Christ's teaching on the Law of Moses (in Matthew) as inapplicable today (for Gentiles), and subscribe only to the Genesis 2 (Mark/Luke) teaching. But this doesn't get rid of the difficulty - is there an exception or isn't there? If we imagine ourselves *as the Jewish disciples*[1] (Matt 23:1-3), was Christ teaching that there was an exceptive clause or wasn't he? In any event, should we reject the moral teaching of the Law? Genesis is as much part of the Law, as Deuteronomy, so is the Law itself contradictory?[2]

2) A second proposal is to say that Genesis defines the ideal standard, but Deuteronomy shows that a concession can be made to human weakness. Christ's emphasis is that 'from the beginning it was not [meant to be] so' (Matt 19:8). And this comment shows some sort of lessening of the application of Genesis by Moses.

This leaves open the question of whether the exceptive clause and Genesis 2 are together applicable today.[3]

The second proposal seems the most satisfactory. At this point we must introduce the principle of concession and covering of sin (Ps 32:1). As a consequence of the Fall, human beings are weak failing creatures. It has been a feature of God's dealings with men that He has overlooked sin (Acts 17:30); he has been longsuffering towards sin (Rms 3:25); and He has made concessions to human weakness. In the

---

[1] Remember Christ was building the church from the beginning of his ministry; if Peter had wanted to get a divorce at this time because of unfaithfulness on the part of his wife, what would Christ have taught?
[2] This is a crucial question. It is too easy a tactic to dismiss Deut 24 by saying that we are not under the Law of Moses. For a Bible student, the question is why Deuteronomy contains an exception and Genesis 2 does not have one. This is a dilemma that is not solved by the fact that we live in Christian times rather than Mosaic times.
[3] It is interesting to observe that Christ's focus is on the position of the person putting asunder and the status of *their* re-marriage. The re-marriage law of Deut 24 is about the position of the one who is put away and the status of their re-marriage(s). This allows the formal suggestion that re-marriage was allowed for the one put away, if this had been done for fornication, but re-marriage was not allowed in any circumstances for the one initiating the divorce.

case of divorce, human hearts have been hardened and unwilling to obey, and hence, Moses *suffered* the practise of divorce among the people.[1] Of course, where there is marital fornication, there should be forgiveness of the failing partner, as often happened in God's relationship with Israel, but sometimes this doesn't follow.

If the acknowledgement of divorce by the Law has been withdrawn for Christians, then there must be a reason for this change. Has human nature become stronger? Has God placed upon Christians a higher moral code, than the one he placed on Israel? This latter point is a common suggestion. But in respect of divorce and re-marriage, he *can't* have placed a higher moral code upon Christians, because Genesis 2 was part of the Law of Moses and placed there for Israel to take instruction. *Israel have always had the highest standard.* Has the N.T. withdrawn the Mosaic concession for Christians?

Christ came to fulfil the Law, and not destroy it, and so, *prima facia*, we would have to have a good reason for rejecting moral principles in the Law. It is in the Sermon on the Mount that Christ delivers his own sayings about what the scribes had taught about the Law. The righteousness of those who would be his disciples had to exceed that of the Scribes and Pharisees. And his disciples today look to this sermon for guidance. It is significant therefore that the *proper interpretation* of Deut 24 features in the sermon. There is no language of Christ that specifically withdraws the Mosaic concession. Christ could have said 'It has been said of old that you may divorce for fornication, but I say unto you that from the beginning it was not meant to be so and you must not divorce'. But we don't have such teaching.

In Matthew 19, Christ replies to the disciples response to his interpretation of Deuteronomy 24, 'If the case of the man be so with his wife, it is not good to marry' (v10), by saying, 'All cannot receive this saying, save they to whom it is given' (v11, cf. 1 Cor 7:7). This seems to indicate that the standard will only be achieved by some, and it seems to be an acknowledgement that some will fail even this approach to marriage.

---

[1] That is, Moses (not the Law?) allowed divorce, and the Law (not Moses?) legislated on re-marriage.

Christ has said that re-marriage after divorce may lead to adultery. The disciples agree (?) to this by saying that in which case it is not good to re-marry. Christ then says that not all can uphold his saying, only those to whom it is 'given'. Does this mean his saying is given to all believers and they will be strengthened to uphold it, or is it that only some believers will be able to uphold his saying? The idea of any concession being made may be discarded by some, but this may be because they fear others will take a concession as a license to sinful behaviour.

We could avoid this idea of concession altogether by applying Christ's remark to eunuchs. But this seems wrong for several reasons. The concession is about a **saying**. The disciples haven't just uttered a saying, since they say that 'it is not good to marry'. Christ was a teacher who had authority to deliver *sayings*, and he often said 'I say unto you...' (Matt 19:9). In Matthew 5 Christ utters a series of *sayings* contrasting them with what was *said of old*, one of these sayings concerns marriage, and is identical to the saying that Christ has just uttered to the Pharisees. So it would seem best to apply the concession to his **marriage sayings**. The remark about eunuchs is not a saying, but rather a comparison centred on everyone's differing ability for celibacy, and Christ makes the concession before his remark about eunuchs.

Concession needs to be balanced with discipline and judgement, but it ought not to be cast aside just because some will take advantage. The forgiveness of God, His mercy and His longsuffering are extended to us just as He concedes that we are weak failing creatures, unprofitable servants. And yet He is and remains a God of judgement, by no means clearing the guilty. Somehow we have to apply the perfect wisdom of God in the day to day affairs of the ecclesia.

The Teaching of Paul

If we wanted to, we could discard the teaching of the Law in Deuteronomy. If we wanted to rid ourselves of the question as to whether Matthew 5 and 19 apply today, we would only have to say that these were comments on the Law, and the Law has nothing to do with *us*. If we wanted *just Christian teaching* on the subject of marriage and divorce, we might place ourselves solely in the hands of Paul. So what *did* Paul say about this subject?

His key comments are found in 1 Cor 7, a chapter much debated -

- the married were not to depart from each other, i.e. divorce each other,[1] but if they did, they were to remain unmarried with a view to reconciliation (1 Cor 7:10-11).

This is a command 'of the Lord' (1 Cor 7:10), but the command is expressed with a parenthesis:

> "Let not the wife depart[2] from her husband, (but and if she depart, let her remain unmarried, or be reconciled to her husband), and let not the husband put away his wife" 1 Cor 7:10b-11

I suggest the presence of the parenthesis because 'Let not the wife depart from her husband...and let not the husband put away his wife' is a re-statement of the *Lord's* command 'let not man (or woman) put asunder', whereas the counsel about remaining unmarried is not part of any of Christ's commands.[3] (Note that Paul doesn't include the aspect of adultery in his instruction here, whereas Christ did talk about this complication).

It would appear that this command of Paul faces two ways. The wife who departs is to remain 'unmarried' and yet she still has a 'husband' with whom she ought to be reconciled. How is it that she can be

---

[1] There is no special word in Greek for a divorce. In English we have the technical verb 'to divorce'. But this is not so in Greek. In 1 Cor 7:10-11, the Greek for 'to depart' is *choridzo* and it is the verb used in Matt 19:6 and Mk 10:9 for 'put asunder'. So although the verb is an ordinary non-technical word for separation, it is clearly used with the meaning of divorce, as the Gospel background shows.

[2] The Greek indicates that the one departing takes the action. An analogous (Aorist passive) use of the Greek is Acts 18:1, where Paul is the one departing from Athens.

[3] Paul is picking up 'let not' and 'man' and substituting for 'man' words for wife and husband, he is also picking up the same Greek word for 'put asunder' in 'let not the wife depart', although he uses a different Greek word for 'put away' in 'let not the husband put away'.

'unmarried' and yet have a husband? Paul evidently recognises that she *could* have married, because he forbids such a second marriage; but he still views her ex-husband as her husband! The dilemma is illusory. The wife who departs evidently divorces her husband, but as now, so too then, the divorced man is termed 'husband' in certain contexts. Sometimes, in our day, a prefix is added like 'ex-husband' or 'former husband', but in the context of describing the *getting of a divorce*, the divorced man might still be called 'your husband'.[1]

In the middle of a command of the Lord, there is a recognition that the command might be disobeyed, and counsel is given to cater for the disobedience. No action on fellowship is advised in Paul's treatment of these marital matters.

We might think that Paul's teaching is not based on the Law of Moses, but he invokes the Law:

> "The wife is bound by the Law as long as her husband liveth; but if her husband be dead, she is at liberty to be married to whom she will; only in the Lord." 1 Cor 7:39

And as with the Law, Paul recognises that there may be divorce, and as with the Law he advises that there should be no second marriage (the Law had said that a second marriage was a cause for moral defilement). It would appear therefore that Christians ought to accept that there may be divorcees among their number.[2]

So if we wanted *'purely Christian'* teaching on this subject, we will not find such a thing with Paul. His comments reinforce the Genesis principle and take into account the practise of divorce that

---

[1] Its worth observing that a *description* of the woman's state as *unmarried* conveys unambiguous information, whereas the man she has divorced can be *referred to* with the term 'husband' *without* implying the information that he is married to his *former* wife. Further, it is a *state* of being unmarried, so that there *has been* a divorce. Paul does not say, 'let her not marry', but rather, 'let her **remain** *unmarried*'.

[2] Some argue that 1 Tim 3:2 and Tit 1:6 indicate this, but this is only one of several possible interpretations of these texts.

Deuteronomy 24 mentions.[1] This means that all the commands about marriage and divorce in the N.T. are set within a framework of the Law of Moses, and both Genesis and Deuteronomy are involved. Christians may not be *under* the Law, but the apostles used the Law to teach a proper way of life. It follows therefore that we can't oppose Christian teaching and the teaching of the Law and select the Christian teaching. Our Christian teaching here originates within the framework of the Law.

Christian Marriage	Mixed Marriage
But and if she depart, let her remain unmarried, or be reconciled to her husband	But if the unbelieving depart, a brother or sister is not under bondage in such cases

The counsel for 'mixed marriages' was the same. The believer was not to put away the unbelieving partner (defined as in 1 Cor 6:6), but if the unbelieving partner divorced the believing partner, the believer was not to regard himself as 'bound' to the unbeliever. It would appear that the believer's function was to sanctify the unbelieving spouse by the washing of the word (1 Cor 6:11, Eph 5:26) and thereby possibly save their partner (v16). In such a relationship the believer is 'bound' to a person who represents that which needs to be cleansed (sin), thus he/she is in bondage to 'sin' (cf. Exodus typology),[2] unless the unbeliever departs. . .

Should we contrast the departure of the unbeliever with the departure of the Christian wife? If we make this contrast, it will mean that there is a permission for re-marriage in the case of breakdown in a mixed marriage. Such a permission would be in the spirit of the recognition of divorce and re-marriage in the Law.

---

[1] The Law regulated the re-marriage to the first husband, and Paul commands against re-marriage. This command that 'she should remain unmarried' reflects the female orientation of Deut 24, and indeed it reflects the view that any second marriage is a cause of moral defilement preventing re-marriage to the first husband.

[2] The typology of sin and cleansing is not out of place in marriage instructions - e.g. Paul advocates that in believer-believer marriage a wife ought to be *reconciled* to her husband - i.e. he uses a verb of atonement.

Paul's counsel regarding marriage and divorce prior to conversion follows his advice about mixed marriages (1 Cor 7:24ff). The general proposal is that a man ought to remain in the condition in which he found himself when he was called (1 Cor 7:24). For the present situation (near to the end of the world), it was good for a man to be as follows: those bound to a wife shouldn't seek to be loosed. Those divorced from a wife shouldn't seek a wife (1 Cor 7:27-28); but if a marriage was contracted after a pre-conversion divorce, such had not sinned (1 Cor 7:28). Paul's general counsel for virgins who converted to Christianity was that they could marry.

Let us summarise our findings:

- The Law of Moses *taught* that marriage was for life and that divorce was not permissible for any cause (Genesis 2).

- It also regulated for re-marriage of the first husband to the first wife. And in the text of this regulation, the Law *acknowledged* the practise of divorce among the people, and that this was for sexual immorality. It acknowledged the practise of divorce in at least first and second marriages, and the cause of such divorces cannot therefore be restricted to sex before marriage.

- There is no right to divorce in the Law, there is no permission. There is no general right for re-marriage for the divorced person or the divorcing person. But the Law acknowledged that divorce was taking place, and it was 'suffered' by Moses. Therefore, the Law sought to regulate re-marriage for the first husband.

- The only O.T. case law we have on the subject of divorce is that of God who gave Israel a bill of divorcement, and this was for sexual immorality, during marriage. This example defines *part* of the scope of the 'matter of nakedness' in Deut 24.

- Jesus' teaching on divorce reflected both Genesis and Deuteronomy. The Matthew teaching reflects Deuteronomy and the Mark/Luke teaching reflects Genesis. If there is a contradiction between the Matthew teaching and the Mark/Luke teaching, then there must be a contradiction between Genesis and Deuteronomy. But there is no such contradiction. It is wrong to try and resolve the 'apparent' contradiction by rejecting the Matthew teaching and adopting the Mark/Luke teaching.

- We cannot reject the Matthew teaching and adopt only the Mark/Luke teaching by saying that the Matthew teaching is just about the Law and it's not applicable to Christians. Genesis is as much a part of the Law as Deuteronomy. By adopting only the Mark/Luke teaching, we would still be adopting the teaching of the Law.

- The best approach to the apparent contradiction is to say that divorce was *acknowledged* under the Law. It would appear to be *acknowledged* for Christians.

- Paul's framework for counsel on divorce and marriage was the Law. We cannot avoid the Law as the setting for our teaching on this matter. He gave advice on Christian marriage and divorce, mixed marriage and divorce, and pre-conversion marriage and divorce.

- For Christian marriage, divorce was forbidden, but it was recognised that a woman might depart from her husband. In such cases, she was to remain unmarried. For mixed marriage, if the unbelieving partner departed, the believer was not bound to that partner, and might then re-marry. For pre-conversion marriage and divorce, a person divorced prior to accepting Christ could re-marry in the Lord.

This is a summary of Biblical teaching. Those who have considered this subject in any depth will appreciate the pitfalls in trying to summarize the subject in this way. I have avoided getting bogged down in the detail of the Bible verses. I have avoided arguments about Greek and Hebrew. I have instead tried to weigh the arguments that are found in the literature and present a balanced case that reflects the standard of Genesis 2 and follows Deuteronomy 24 in acknowledging that the children of God will fail and disobey.

Fellowship

Fellowship is a thorny problem, and this is because it involves a person's whole *being*. This is particularly true for Christadelphians, who have come out of the world and come out of the churches around them. Furthermore, **the truth** as an entity is of utmost importance to the Christadelphian. They have committed their life to the truth and upholding the truth, and a great deal of emotional energy is bound up with keeping the truth in opposition to the churches around. Consequently, there are many divisions, and many of these have been over matters of divorce and re-marriage. However, zeal for the truth has to be tempered with forbearance and longsuffering.

In this section, we have only one question: how do we handle disagreement over divorce and re-marriage? Should like-minded ecclesias group together and form 'fellowships', i.e. distinct autonomous and *competing churches*, or should divorce and re-marriage be handled within the body of Christ by allowing *ecclesias* to autonomously determine their own practise?

Inter-ecclesial Standards
With respect to divorce and re-marriage, should there be one policy across the ecclesias? The short answer is, 'Yes!'. (Compare the lessons of Acts 15, which show that the 'apostles' among us must strive for inter-ecclesial unity). But what if there isn't one policy? What if there has been faulty leadership? Should ecclesias give up on each other and divide up into groups that are like minded on divorce and re-marriage? There are several things to consider when answering this question:

Firstly, what ecclesial discipline should be applied to those who contravene the guidelines on marriage? Should there be one disciplinary policy across all ecclesias? What are the commands concerning discipline to apply in such cases?

Secondly, can we be sure that the scriptural statements on divorce and re-marriage are clear cut? Is there room for genuine disagreement amongst mature brethren?

Thirdly, do the Scriptures cover all the cases that present themselves today, or are the Scriptures being applied and extended to meet new situations, and are these applications of Scripture the source of disagreement?

Fourthly, is it doctrinally possible to block divide the body of Christ on a divorce and re-marriage question? Can we disregard the doctrine of unity around the Gospel in Christ?

These are difficult questions, because things can go too far. Genuine disagreement exists between Christadelphians and other churches, but it would be folly to propose that Christadelphians should forget their differences with other churches just because those in other churches are quite sincere. But then, let us remember that the differences between Christadelphians and other churches have to do with the Gospel, whereas disagreement among Christadelphians on marriage and divorce is a disagreement amongst *brethren of Christ* who agree on the Gospel.

Scriptural teaching is clear, but clarity is in the eye of the beholder. I have set out my views, but there are other positions. Some argue *any* divorce followed by re-marriage is adultery, and if this *is* so, it is certain that adulterers cannot be in fellowship (e.g. Gal 5:19-21, Eph 5:3-7). Some argue that divorce and re-marriage is possible in certain circumstances, for example, when there has been adultery by one partner. Some argue that re-marriage is possible when the original marriage can no longer be rescued, perhaps due to the marriage of one of the original spouses. Yet others say re-marriage is possible only if there is genuine repentance and recognition that the divorce was wrong. Can these different views be accommodated within one body?

Such views exist across fellowships, and fellowship is fractured as a result. There are two types of fracture: there is the 'block' division between separate and autonomous fellowships. Each fellowship holds fast to the same head, but otherwise they have nothing to do with each other. And there is the messier type of fracture whereby local ecclesias in a fellowship disagree over a divorce or re-marriage matter and relationships break down in some way.

Which, *if* any, is the better situation? One strategy makes a clean break with all who disagree with the stance being adopted. A competing church is set up as a result. The other strategy sees ecclesias fracture relationships while remaining formally part of the same fellowship. The hope is that over time the disagreements will be resolved.

The question that needs to be posed at this point is whether we can, *as men*, divide the body of Christ on the matter of divorce and remarriage. We argued in Chapter Two that the Gospel was the basis of faith because it was the means by which God was building the church. Can we go against this and divide the church on a ground that does not affect the Gospel? Of course, if the Gospel is challenged, then the body must be protected through separation.

It is not as if the positive teaching on marriage within the wider brotherhood differs that much across fellowships. The commands of Christ in this respect are taught, and the Edenic ideal is stressed. The disagreement occurs because ecclesias disagree over what to do when there is marital failure. When this happens, the temptation exists to push the Gospel to one side and forget about it, concentrate on the disagreement, and withdraw fellowship from all who refuse to acknowledge your position.

Repentance
Repentance lies at the heart of fellowship. The clarion call of John the Baptist, of Jesus and the apostles was 'Repent, and be baptized for the remission of sins'. Without repentance there could be no baptism, no remission of sins, and no participation in Christ and the Abrahamic promises. Repentance is the beginning of the process of conversion - (Acts 2:38, 9:35, 11:21,15:19, 26:20). Because repentance has this foundational role, it is properly part of the basis of fellowship. A man comes to Christ, and regardless of his past life, regardless of the sins he has committed, provided he repents, he can be accepted (Prov 28:13).

What is this repentance? Sin can be identified, it is transgression of God's law (1 Jn 3:4), and we have a record of that law. If sin can be identified, then repentance can be identified. Such repentance is not just a state of mind, though it is certainly *that* - instead we should see it as a state of mind reflected in behaviour. It is made up of behaviour of various kinds. A lot of the behaviour involved in repentance is verbal and conversational. The sort of verbal behaviour that makes up repentance might be anything from a simple apology to the distraught confession of sin seen in the case of David.

It is important to see that repentance has many facets. It is perhaps easier to see this when we think of *life as a whole*, but repentance of any *one particular sin or characteristic in a life* will also show itself in various ways. We can't often make a simple equation between repentance and some *one act* of repentance. This is possible sometimes, but not always, and the more deeply embedded the structure of sin in a person's life, the more we will find it impossible to pin-point some **one act of repentance** that is sufficient and appropriate. Just as sin is all pervading, so too repentance may need to be all pervading.

If sin is completely forsaken, it is forsaken in all behaviours. But repentance of sin is very often only partial and incomplete. For example, none of the good reforming kings of Judah succeeded in completely purifying the nation of idol worship, the nation only partially repented, yet God continued to work with them. Or again, there were many exhortations of the apostles to 'put off the old man', and these were made to those of many years in the faith.

A man who repents will forsake his sin in some way. On the other hand, there will be structures in his life, which are sinful, and which he will not be able to forsake straightaway. He will find himself going back to sin. Even for particular aspects of his life, he will find himself failing (Rms 7:14-21). Repentance is never a complete forsaking of all sins, and for some particular sin it may never be complete. What then about the situation where a person displays some behaviours indicating repentance but not others? How do we judge repentance?

It is part of the conflict between the spirit and the flesh that we suffer lower standards of achievement. Those who argue that a complete forsaking is always possible and always necessary for fellowship are usually concerned with external appearances. But this seems to reflect a 'catholic' desire for a single corresponding act of penance to correspond to the original sin, and a desire for a show of purity. But Biblical repentance is not like that, because it is concerned first with the heart and how a change of heart is showing itself throughout the whole of a person's life in various behaviours (Hos 6:6). Once we look into the heart and see its true nature (Jer 17:9), we learn that repentance of even the smallest individual sin is tainted with failure (Is 64:6). We are all in the process of forsaking our thoughts and ways and adopting those of God.

If repentance stands at the beginning of the Christian life (Is 55:7), it should also feature throughout that life. This is because we all sin throughout life. The argument about fellowship here is straightforward: if repentance is a condition of entry to the church, it should be seen as a condition of *continued membership* of the church, should a person sin. We cannot ply the argument that we can sin in order that grace might abound. Unrepented sin is a denial of the authority of God over our lives. Hence, for those out of fellowship, if they seek fellowship once again, there should be repentance of the behaviour that led to their exclusion from the community. It's like a 'new' entry into the church.

Any discussion of the standards of repentance must recognize these two principles:

- we must acknowledge that God recognizes *degrees of repentance* in his children. Repentance is never absolute in respect of our lives. We each illustrate repentance in the fruit we bear, but we each offer up different yields, thus showing that repentance and forsaking of the flesh is not complete. Furthermore, any discussion of the standards of repentance must acknowledge the difficulty of laying down in advance exactly what counts as repentance. We can only say at the *theoretical level* that there must be some fruits meet for repentance in the aspect of life we are considering. It is difficult to lay down such standards, because repentance is not a theoretical matter. Repentance is intimately related to the circumstances and life of each individual.

- we also need to recognize that while God sets an absolute standard (Matt 5:48), He accepts a lower standard of achievement. He does this because of the abiding presence of faith in our hearts. If we continue to have faith in Christ, then God will forgive our many shortcomings.

As a result, we must apply the spiritual wisdom that we have developed to cases of divorce and re-marriage and judge each case as it arises. Such wisdom comes from many years reading and thinking about the Scriptures. It's a wisdom drawn from all parts of the Bible, and from all the evidence that we have about *how* God has dealt with His people.

Repentance and Marital Failure
What standards of repentance should we apply for those seeking baptism? What standards of repentance do we apply in those seeking re-fellowship? The man of the world is under no obligation to serve God, and he has been ignorant of God's requirements. When he comes to Christ, he repents of his former way of life, but former sins may not be undone. Is it different for brethren and sisters who fall? They were under an obligation to the commands of Christ. They had knowledge and were responsible to their Lord and Master. If they sin, are their conditions of repentance more stringent than the unbaptised convert?

In this context we can consider marriage and divorce. What are the standards of repentance in cases of divorce? The issue here is whether or not to apply the standard that the divorce or the second marriage should be completely forsaken. This issue has divided Christadelphians. Again the choice is a simple one: is the divorcee to re-constitute the marriage if he is able; or again, is the re-married person to divorce the second spouse and perhaps re-marry the first spouse, regardless of any children in the first or second marriage? Or can the sins of divorce and re-marriage be forsaken in a manner that falls short of the restitution of the original marriage? What if a person is truly sorry that he has divorced his spouse, and he shows this in many ways, but is not willing to re-marry the spouse?

In the case of divorce and re-marriage, these failures are continuing *states*. A man who is angry or spiteful may sin, but the sin is momentary compared with the failings of a divorce, a re-marriage, or a marrying out of the faith. These are enduring states, and as such, they are like the enduring features of character that a person has, such as a tendency to be angry, or a tendency to be greedy. We all have enduring characteristics that are fleshly, and they are manifested in specific sins. We are all good at describing each other's characteristic faults, but we are curiously blind to our distinctive failings. What standards of repentance should we apply to our distinctive failings?

There are two problem-areas here: one concerns whether the correct standard of repentance is or is not complete forsaking; the other problem-area is whether we can allow repentance to fall short of complete forsaking. Let us look at these issues with regard to divorce first, and then re-marriage.

Those who argue that complete forsaking of a divorce ideally requires the original marriage to be restored are correct. Paul suffered divorce, but he counselled reconciliation. However, no time-scale is placed on the reconciliation, nor any order of events. There must be evidence that the divorce is acknowledged to be wrong, and that reconciliation is sought. But there is no stipulation that restoration of the original marriage is a condition of fellowship.

However, those who argue that re-constituting the original marriage is *alone sufficient* to count as a *complete forsaking* of the original sin, put forward a superficial view. A marriage may be re-constituted *in name*, but there might be all sorts of underlying and hidden behaviours which show that the spirit of the marriage has not been restored. Although the divorce is mended *on paper*, in a person's heart it may be alive.

Perhaps the correct standard is complete forsaking of a divorce, but can we give way to lower standard of achievement? Here the Bible shows us that we must, if necessary, *suffer* a lower standard of achievement (e.g. Matt 19:10), in the hope that a person will in time bring forth further fruits meet for repentance.

As regards re-marriage, the situation is more complex. The Law of Moses regulated *against* restoring a first marriage if there had been a second marriage, because the second marriage was regarded as a cause of defilement (Deut 24:1-4). The counsel of Paul was that a woman should remain unmarried, and this is consistent with the objective of avoiding any defilement from a second marriage. But if a woman (or a man) contracts a second marriage, should this second marriage be undone, whether or not there are children, if they are to be in fellowship? We have no Biblical cases of second marriage to consider. It seems reasonable to follow the example of the Law and say that the original marriage must *not* be restored if there have been intervening second marriages. But should the second marriage be annulled, even though the first marriage cannot be restored? Should there be a further divorce of a second marriage, regardless of whether there are any children of that marriage?

Failure and Longsuffering
The principle to lay alongside repentance is a principle of failure and longsuffering. We commit sin, and for this we need the forbearance and longsuffering of God. Hence Paul says,

> "Or despisest thou the riches of his goodness and forbearance and longsuffering; not knowing that the goodness of God leadeth thee to repentance?" Rms 2:4

The point Paul is making is that the forbearance and longsuffering of God (His goodness) are ways of leading a person to repentance. In God's dealings with man, He is patient and through this He seeks to lead a man to repent (1 Pet 3:20). He is not slack concerning His promises, but He is longsuffering, not wishing that any should perish, but that all should come to repentance (2 Pet 3:9). Such forbearance and longsuffering are features of the atonement. The sins of former times had been passed over in a spirit of forbearance, so that God might exhibit His righteousness in Christ (Rms 3:25).
The point for us is that we ought to imitate this example. The problem is that if we do, it will mean for a time suffering the presence of sin in the walk of a fellow believer. This already happens quite a lot, because we are taught to forbear one another in love. And don't we 'put up with' each other's failings in a spirit of quiet resignation sometimes? We should seek the best in each other, but we will need to be patient if we seek immediate results.

The fruit of the spirit is longsuffering (Gal 5:22), and we are counselled to 'put on' longsuffering, tender mercy and kindness as a garment (Col 3:12). A characteristic of Paul's ministry was 'much patience' and longsuffering (2 Cor 6:4,6). A servant of the Lord must be apt to teach and be patient (2 Tim 2:24). This was the example of our High Priest. He was taken from among men so that he might have compassion on the ignorant and on those who are going astray (Hebs 5:2).

The principle of failure and longsuffering is reinforced by the fact that we all differ in ability and strength to serve God. There are those who are weak and those who are strong, and people are weak and strong at different times in their lives.

The parable of the sower is a familiar parable, but one feature is often overlooked. The seed that is sown into 'good' ground gives **different yields**. Indeed some ground is only thirty percent productive, seventy percent is unproductive (such people would be sacked by any half decent company - such are the ways of man). The seed is the word of God, and the fruits of the ground that are worth harvesting are the fruits of the spirit. But the disciples of Christ are different in what they can achieve, there are different degrees of success and failure.

Another parable with a similar point is the parable of the pounds. To each servant the master gave a sum of money *according to his ability*. And there was a corresponding return. The servant with ten pounds doubled his monies; the servant with only one pound did nothing, because he was afraid. The point here is that some have greater or lesser ability to work in the service of the master. It is a similar point to that of the parable of the sower - the ground gives different yields. Both parables show something about performance - this will vary from individual to individual. How do we apply this today? There are two possibilities. People will do more or less in the vineyard, this is one way to apply the parables. Another view is that people will have greater or less success in their personal walks before God.

Spiritual performance is about *bearing fruit*. We are to bring forth fruits meet for repentance (Matt 3:8), and the fruits we bring forth show in what aspects of our life we have repented. But this is a life-long process, and the Lord looks from year to year to see what fruit we bring forth in our lives (Lk 13:7). Indeed, even when he might cut us down, he allows us a further chance to repent and bring forth fruit (Lk 13:8). And the quantity of fruit we bear will differ from person to person. Only if we do not yield *any* fruit will we be cut down (Matt 3:10, Lk 13:9).

There is therefore a principle of stronger and weaker in the faith, there is a principle of varying degrees of spiritual understanding, and there is a principle of growth in Christ. These principles mean that we have to be very careful how we judge our fellow brethren. They also mean that we have to exercise patience and longsuffering towards each other in respect of our failings, both our moral lapses and our spiritual dimness.

Paul spoke to those who were 'dull of hearing' and unskilful in the word. He addressed those who needed milk when they should have been taking meat (Hebs 5:11-13). These were apparently believers who had not grown from babes to maturity in the time that Paul had expected. What the example shows is that some will have a lack of knowledge, and they will need to be taught and not dismissed.

Conclusion
We all have a conscience. Brethren and Sisters are at different stages in their spiritual growth, and each may have a different view of the question of divorce and re-marriage. This may change over time. A staunch advocate of one position in early years may mellow with the passing of time. Conflict and disagreement polarises the mind, and the agreements that exist (on the Gospel) get pushed to the background.

What should we do about our consciences? It can be abused. People of the world, and in other religions, exercise *their* conscience in ways with which we would part company, so the conscience is not necessarily always 'right'. In the children of God, the conscience is the expression of the will of the spiritual man in conflict with the flesh. It needs to be developed and tutored. There can't be anybody in the Western world today who is terribly worried about whether the meat bought in a supermarket has been anywhere near a shrine, and yet in Paul's day, this was a question that bothered people's conscience; it was an issue that caused people to leave the community.

There are principles in the 'meat offered to idols' case. The first principle is a *lack of knowledge*. Within the community there were some who hadn't quite grasped the doctrine that there was one God (!), they hadn't carried this through to the conclusion that idols were nothing. They ate meat thinking it had been offered to a local god, and they went against their own conscience. Our consciences are informed by our beliefs. And if we have a faulty understanding of some things, our conscience may be likewise affected. This was the case in Corinth. They had a faulty belief among their set of beliefs and this belief informed their conscience that eating meat offered to local deities was wrong. As a result their conscience was defiled. It is the same with us. Faulty beliefs can inform our conscience, and lead us to take actions.

A second point is that brethren with the faulty beliefs were weak. Those with the correct beliefs were to take heed lest they cause the weaker brethren to stumble and fall away. There is here a practical example of forbearance - forbearing those with a wrong notion (doctrine). Paul doesn't address the weak brethren directly, as if to say, 'come on, isn't it obvious that an idol is nothing', and leave it at that - no, he says that idols are nothing, but he lays it upon the stronger ones to exercise patience and wait for the weaker ones to see the truth more clearly.

Whether we are weak or strong, we need to *love* one another. The first casualty of division is *love*. Brethren and sisters go their separate ways. Time passes and children are born. They grow up and have little to do with others in different fellowships. And so fellowships become competing churches. The body remains divided. But we shouldn't abandon the ideal of unity; we must strive for this goal in the body of Christ. Neither should we abandon the principles of Christ, and in particular, the standard of one man and one woman for life. We must uphold this standard even as we go forward in dialogue with all of the body, always trying to seek each other's good above our own.